A POETIC TREASURY FROM BELARUS

A celebration of the life and work of Vera Rich

Editors
Jim Dingley
Revd David Parry

London 2019

HERTFORDSHIRE PRESS

Printed by Hertfordshire Press Ltd © 2019
e-mail: publisher@hertfordshirepress.com
www.hertfordshirepress.com

A POETIC TREASURY
FROM BELARUS
A celebration of the life and work of Vera Rich

Editors: Jim Dingley & Revd David Parry

supported by:

European Bank
for Reconstruction and Development

*British Library Catalogue in Publication Data
A catalogue record for this book is available from the British Library
Library of Congress in Publication Data
A catalogue record for this book has been requested*

ISBN: 978-1-913356-04-0

CONTENTS

INTRODUCTION

This book has a twofold purpose. The first is to introduce just some of the riches of the literature of Belarus to a new generation of English speakers. This is a process that was begun by the poet and translator Vera Rich (1936-2009) in her UNESCO-supported book *Like Water, Like Fire: An anthology of Byelorussian poetry from 1828 to the present day* (London: George Allen & Unwin Ltd., 1972).

The second purpose is to celebrate Vera's life and work on the tenth anniversary of her death. This book concentrates on the three poets whose work provided the foundations upon which modern Belarusian literature has been built: Janka Kupala, the prophet of Belarus; Jakub Kolas, the recorder of Belarusian life; and Maksim Bahdanovič, the outstanding lyricist. It includes both the Belarusian originals and Vera's translations. There is a brief introductory essay on each poet. The essay on Kupala is written by Prof. Viačaslaŭ Rahojša of the Belarusian State University in Minsk, whose wide-ranging research has focussed on the three poets and their impact on literature and society in the twentieth century. The essays on Kolas and Bahdanovič were provided by Arnold McMillin, Professor Emeritus of the School of Slavonic and East European Studies, University College London, whose academic association with Belarus began in the 1960s and continues right up to the present day. All three essays mention the newspaper *Naša Niva* (Our Cornfield). It was the first Belarusian newspaper, published between 1906 and 1915 in Vilnia (now Vilnius, the capital of modern Lithuania) and revived in 1991 in Minsk.

The special feature of this book is that it presents translations made by Vera which have not previously been published in this country, *eg* Kupala's sonnets that were originally written in Belarusian (earlier ones were written in Polish), sections of Kolas' epic *The New Land* translated after the appearance of her anthology, and one crucial poem by Bahdanovič ('Pahonia', The Chase).

Vera Rich as translator of Belarusian literature
One of the obituaries that appeared after her death is entitled 'Vera Rich – translator, journalist, poet and human rights activist'. She indeed played all these roles: as journalist she wrote expertly on science in the Soviet Union, and – after 1986 – especially on the Chernobyl nuclear accident and its aftermath; her first published works were translations from Polish, Ukrainian and Old Norse, and three volumes of her own poetry; she founded the poetry group 'Manifold'; she was a fierce defender of free speech, especially in Poland and those parts of the USSR with which she felt a special bond in the 1980s.

She discovered Belarus in the 1950s through her contact with the Belarusian Uniate (Greek Catholic) Chapel in Finchley, North London. This developed into a lifelong association with the Belarusian community in the UK. After the declaration of independence of the Republic of Belarus in 1991 Vera was at long last able freely to visit the country that had captured her imagination, and establish a close friendship with Prof. Rahojša, as well as with many contemporary writers.

Vera brought her keen poetic sense of the English language to bear in her versions of the Belarusian originals.

The structure of the book
The sections devoted to the poetry of Kolas and Bahdanovič both have notes that were written by Vera herself for inclusion in the 1972 anthology. I have provided notes for those parts of Kolas' *The New Land* that were translated after 1972, and for the poem 'Pahonia' by Bahdanovič. To the best of my knowledge Vera did not provide any notes to her translations of Kupala's sonnets. There is an appendix that serves as a record of some of Vera's visits to Belarus.

Acknowledgements
First and foremost, thanks are due to the European Bank for Reconstruction and Development for their indispensable financial assistance. I am grateful to the Embassy of the Republic of Belarus in London, in particular to His Excellency Ambassador Sergei Aleinik, and to Minister-Counsellor Aleg Yermalovich for their encouragement and support. Without them and Alison Cameron, a longstanding friend of Vera's, this book would have been unthinkable. I thank Marat Akhmedjanov and the Hertfordshire Press for their patience and for publishing the book. The trustees of the Francis Skaryna Belarusian Library and Museum in London hold the copyright to Vera's translations from Belarusian; I am especially grateful to them for their continued support.

I owe a particular debt of gratitude to Prof. Rahojša for his invaluable suggestions and advice, and for his careful reading and, where necessary, amendment of the Belarusian texts of the poems. I am grateful to Prof. McMillin for contributing essays on Kolas and Bahdanovič, and to Maryja Mickievič, the granddaughter of Jakub Kolas, for entrusting to me Vera's manuscript translations of sections of *The New Land* that were made after 1972.

Last, but most certainly not least, this book – and so Vera herself – has brought me into contact with David Parry, who I am so pleased to have as co-editor. Working on the book has aroused in him an enthusiasm for Belarusian culture, exactly the kind of result that I am sure Vera was aiming for in her translations.

Jim Dingley
Margate

FOREWORD

Great book with a wonderful collection of Belarusian poetry created by the outstanding Belarusian poets Janka Kupala, Jakub Kolas and Maksim Bahdanovič. Their literary art embraced all the colours of Belarusian land, revealing its uniqueness and beauty. They left an invaluable spiritual heritage, lit by high talent, wisdom, love and kindness to people.

The current edition is an excellent opportunity for the readers to acquaint themselves with the work of these poet-prophets, who foresaw the coming statehood of the Belarusian people and its becoming a full member of the international community.

Preservation and knowledge of the deeply national heritage of Kupala, Kolas and Bahdanovič ensure that the Belarusian language and Belarusian identity will continue to live. And those abroad who want to better understand Belarus will be greatly helped by the talent of the brilliant translator Vera Rich, who sincerely loved our country and Belarusian poetry.

We are very grateful to the editors of the book Jim Dinley and Revd David Parry for their hard work and tenacity, deep knowledge and intellectuality.

Special thanks to the European Bank for Reconstruction and Development for supporting the publication of this book.

Sergei Aleinik
Ambassador of Belarus to the United Kingdom

A BRIEF NOTE ON SPELLING

First: the name of the country itself: following independence the form 'Belarus' has gained general international acceptance, with 'Belarusian' as the derived adjective. Before independence the forms 'Belorussia' and 'Byelorussia' were used.

Second: the Belarusian language is written in the Cyrillic script. However the Latin script has also been used in Belarusian printing since the nineteenth century (some of it in London, incidentally). The use of the Latin script was eventually codified: Vera made use of it in her translations and notes. A modification of this script is in use in Belarus today to render place names, the names of stations on the Minsk metro, and signboards intended for tourists. I have where necessary adjusted Vera's use of Latin-script Belarusian to ensure conformity with modern usage.

Latin script	Cyrillic	English equivalent
C	Ц	an**ts**
Č	Ч	**ch**urch
CH	Х	Scots 'lo**ch**'
H	Г	**h**at (not like Russian!)
I	І	k**ee**n
J	Й	**y**es
Ĺ	ЛЬ	soft 'l'
Ń	НЬ	soft 'n'
Ś	СЬ	soft 's'
Ŭ	ў	**w**et
Y	Ы	b**i**t (almost)
Ź	ЗЬ	soft 'z'
Ž	Ж	mea**s**ure

JANKA KUPALA

Janka Kupala (pseudonym of Ivan Lucevič, 1882-1942) was born in a family of petty tenant farmers on the Viazynka estate near Minsk on 7 July. According to the calendar in use in the Russian Empire before the October Revolution of 1917, this was 25 June: the Summer Solstice, Midsummer's Eve, the Feast of St John the Baptist, known in Belarus as Ivan Kupala. It is no surprise therefore that, when he began to write and publish his works, he chose the pen-name Janka Kupala. He received his primary education in a local school. Then he started work: tenant farmer, brewery labourer, librarian, employee and later editor of a newspaper, student of the evening four-year (1909-1913) general education courses for adults in St Petersburg and of the Evening University in Moscow (1915) - this was the path to knowledge taken by Janka Kupala; in the end, coupled with active self-education, it brought him to the position of academician of two Academies of Sciences – in Belarus and Ukraine.

The first Belarusian writer to receive the title 'National Poet of Belarus' (in 1925), Janka Kupala started out on the road to the heights of creativity in 1905, when the Minsk Russian-language newspaper 'North-Western Region' (as Belarus was then called) published his poem 'Mužyk' (The Peasant). The revolution of 1905-1907 had led to the lifting of a more than a century-old ban on the use of the language in printing, so at that same time his poetry began to appear in Belarusian-language publications, first in the weekly newspaper *Naša Niva* (Vilnia, 1906-1915), where the poet published about 150 verses, one of which was the famous poem 'Kurhan' (The Gravemound; 1912). Then the Belarusian publishing house in St Petersburg, called 'The Sun will shine into our little window

13

too' (1906-1914), published the poet's first collection of verses *Žaliejka* (The Reed-Pipe, 1908). It was in St Petersburg that Janka Kupala prepared and published two more collections of verses: *Huśliar* (The Minstrel, 1910) and *Šliacham žyćcia* (On the Road of Life, 1913), and the dramatic poem 'Adviečnaja pieśnia' (The Eternal Song, 1910). He refined his artistic skill by attending performances in St Petersburg theatres, and so fulfilled his idea of writing dramatic works: the dramatic poem 'Son na kurhanie' (Dream on the gravemound, 1910), and the plays *Paŭlinka* (1912) and *Raśkidanoje hniazdo* (A Scattered Nest, 1913), which, like the later *Tutejšyja* (The Local Folk, 1922), are still staged in Belarusian theatres today.

After 1919 Janka Kupala lived almost permanently in Minsk, and engaged in literary and social work. He wrote the sharp social comedy *Tutejšyja*, and published many poems, several of which are distinctly patriotic, *eg* 'Spadčyna' (Heritage, 1922), 'Arlianatam' (To the Eaglets, 1923) and 'Sychodziš, vioska, z jasnaj javy...' (Thou Passest, Village, from Bright Story..., 1929). Among the verse collections published by Kupala were *Spadčyna* (Heritage, 1922), *Bieznazoŭnaje* (Nameless, 1925), *Ad sierca* (From the heart, 1940). He participated in the creation of the Belarusian State University (1921), the Academy of Sciences of Belarus (1929), and the Writers' Union (1934). However, his life was not always cloudless. In 1930, during the Stalinist repressions, he tried to commit suicide, unable to withstand the baseless accusations aimed at him. On 28 June 1942, Kupala died tragically in the Moscow hotel "Moskva" under mysterious circumstances. He was buried in Moscow's Vagankovo Cemetery. In 1962, the urn with the poet's ashes was reburied in the Minsk Military Cemetery next to the grave of Jakub Kolas.

When summing up the twenty years of his literary activity, Janka Kupala in the poem 'Za ŭsio' (For All, 1926) wrote: "I have repaid my people, // With whatso'er I might, // From slavery called to freedom, // From darkness called to light." From slavery to freedom, from darkness to light... This was the road the poet himself trod together with the Belarusian people. Janka Kupala was undoubtedly an artistic chronicler of the people's life. But he was more than that. At various times, depending on the circumstances, he was a subtle and sincere lyricist transformed into a poet-citizen, a prophet, a philosopher, and even a warrior. His work did not only reflect the growth of the socio-political and national consciousness of Belarusians, but also actively contributed to this growth; it helped the formation of a social ideal and a national identity, it awakened their historical memory and became the banner of the spiritual revival of the people. In 1919-1920 it was Janka Kupala who developed the concept of independent statehood for Belarus; among the articles he wrote on this topic are ones entitled 'Independence', 'An Independent State and its Peoples', 'The Cause of Belarusian Independence over the past year'. His dream of independence for Belarus was realised only in the early 1990s.

Kupala is an outstanding master of poetic language, one of the greatest poets of the Slavonic world. He did more than introduce into Belarusian poetry some previously unknown forms of verse (he wrote the first sonnets in Belarusian), but also created new ones. The poet raised the culture of the Belarusian poem to the world level; like no other Belarusian poet he contributed to the development of the technique of versification, brought original rhythms and intonations to Belarusian poetry, and identified the most promising ways for it to develop in the future.

He is truly a symbol of Belarus.

Prof. Viačaslaŭ Rahojša
Minsk

А хто там ідзе?

А хто там ідзе, а хто там ідзе
У агромністай такой грамадзе?
    — Беларусы.

А што яны нясуць на худых плячах,
На руках у крыві, на нагах у лапцях?
    — Сваю крыўду.

А куды ж нясуць гэту крыўду ўсю,
А куды ж нясуць напаказ сваю?
    — На свет цэлы.

А хто гэта іх, не адзін мільён,
Крыўду несць научыў, разбудзіў іх сон?
    — Бяда, гора.

А чаго ж, чаго захацелась ім,
Пагарджаным век, ім, сляпым, глухім?
    — Людзьмі звацца.

1905—1907

And, say, who goes there?

And, say, who goes there? And, say, who goes there?
In such a mighty throng assembled, O declare!
Belarusians!

And what do those lean shoulders bear as load,
Those hands stained dark with blood,
those feet bast-sandal shod?
All their grievance!

And to what place do they this grievance bear,
And whither do they take it to declare?
To the whole world!

And who schooled them thus, many million strong,
Bear their grievance forth,
roused them from slumbers long?
Want and suffering!

And what is it, then, for which so long they pined,
Scorned throughout the years, they, the deaf, the blind?
To be called human!

SONNETS

Жніво ("Наспелая постаць шчаслівых пасеваў...")

Наспелая постаць шчаслівых пасеваў
За вёскай, на сонным лясоў рубяжы,
Ссівелы ўжо колас схінула к мяжы
У сумным шаптанні: «Дзе, жнеі мае вы?»

І жнеі сышліся.- Направа, налева
Кладучы ў снапы каласы-старажы,
Зашасталі глуха сярпы, як нажы,
Пад жніўныя вечна старыя напевы.

Спагадная, нудная песня плыве,
Губляючы ў пушчы свае пераливы,
У шэлестах белага коласу нівы.

Плыве гэта песня ка мне і заве,
І ў сэрцы звініць, як каса у траве:
«Ты так жа, брат, сееш... а дзе тваё жніва?»

1910

Reaping

The full-ripened figure of fortunate sowings
Past the village, and out to the sleepy woods eaves,
Already grown grey, a grain-ear nods, grieves
Whispers: "Where are you, my reapers? Time's going!"

The reapers came hot-foot - and to-ing and fro-ing,
They gather the guardian ears into sheaves,
Their sickles are clashing like knives, and there weaves
Over them, age-old, the harvest songs flowing.

Plaintively, sadly the song floats away,
Loses its trills where the forest spreads deeply,
In whispers of white ears the tillage is keeping,

And the song floats to me too, comes to say
(In the heart chiming like scythe in the hay):
"You, too, have sowed, brother... Where is your reaping?"

Запушчаны палац

Твой кволы валадар, забыўшыся навук
Велічыні Зыгмунтавай і лет цярпення,
«Раздзел» узаканяе ў загранічным ценю
І лічыць, колькі дома кінуў хвоек штук...

А дома, роскашы і працы многіх рук,
Папас магнацкіх перацвіўшых пакаленняў,
Стаіш,- і цэгла валіцца з гнілых скляпенняў,
І ў шчыліне гняздо ўе ўслужлівы павук.

Жывёлу гоне ў парк галодны «сервітут»,
Ля сцен цянюе забабон ад лета ў лета:
Нячысцік з ведзьмамі гуляе ў пустцы гэтай.

Так зніштажэнне ў кожан гзымс паўзе і кут
І зубы скаліць: «Моц мая і права тут!
На ўход жыцця сюды ўжо я кладу тут «veto»».

1910

The deserted palace

Thy lord enfeebled long since ceased to understand
The lessons of great Sigmund's age, the years of anguish,
«Partition» drove him forth in foreign shade to languish,
Counting the fir-trees back at home on his own land.

And there at home, raised, furbished by so many hands,
The seat of noble generations flowered and vanished,
Bricks falling from thy rotten ceilings, lone thou standest,
And in the cracks the busy spider spins her strands,

The hungry «servitude» drives cattle in the park,
From year to year thy walls are veiled in superstition,
In thy wastes, fiend and coven dance in wild volition,

In every nook and cranny creeps destruction dark,
Gnashing its teeth: «My power and might rule here,
so mark:
No life shall enter 'gainst my veto's prohibition!»

Па межах родных і разорах

Па межах родных і разорах,
Пад небам зводна-неспагадным,
Спакоем воджаны век здрадным,
Сную, і нейкі са мной шорах.

Са мной, за мною ўслед сум-вораг
З глухім нашэптам, непрынадным:
Як ты ні хочаш быць праглядным,-
Сягоння ўсё тут - як і ўчора ж!

Усё жыве тым самым Богам,
Таксама шумнае прадвесне
Усёй не зводзе з гоняў плесні...

Араты ўсход нясе адлогам:
Курган чапаючы нарогам,
Не ўспомніць прадзедавай песні.

1910

Across my native fields and furrows

Across my native fields and furrows,
Under a sky unfriendly, easeless,
Peace of the ages, fraught with treason,
Leads me; I creep, and something follows.

With me, behind me, foeman-sorrow
With dull grim whisper ever teases;
Though to play prophet it may please you:
Today is yesterday's unchanged morrow.

Everything lives by the same God still,
Even spring's herald, loudly ringing,
Cannot cleanse fields from mildew clinging...

Ploughman brings shoots to fallow sod still:
Though ploughshare into gravemounds prods still,
He recalls not ancestral singing.

Для зямлі прадзедаў маіх...

Я табе, зямля мая прадзедаў маіх,
Не патраплю нічога жалець на свеце,
На свет цэлы гатоў твой прыгон апеці
І ўзнясці пасад на магілішчах тваіх.

Я цябе душой рад бы сваёй сагрэці
І карону сплесці з сонца, зор залатых,
На цябе карону ўзлажыць, каб хоць на міг
Заяснела ты ў цяжка дабытым цвеце.

За цябе загінуць гатоў я ў барацьбе
З крыўдай той, што цярпіш ад людзей і Бога,
Ад чужынца і ад сына свайго сляпога...

Буду ў вечнай мучыцца жальбе і кляцьбе...
І за гэта толькі прашу, малю цябе:
Не гані ты мяне ад свайго парога.

1912

For the land of my forebears...

O land of those ancient forebears of mine,
There is naught in the world I'd not hasten to bring thee,
To the whole world I am ready to sing thee,
To raise thee up a throne on those graveyards of thine.

Happily with my soul I would breathe warmth within thee,
Or weave thee a crown from sun and stars' gold shine,
And crown thee with it, though for one moment's time,
For thee to shine in beauty all too hard for winning.

For thee in the fray I'd perish readily,
Against the wrongs heaped on thee by men and God,
unkindly,
By the stranger and by thine own son in his blindness.

I will suffer endless griefs and woes eternally.
And for this I'll seek but one small thing from thee,
That thou'lt not drive me out, but keep me here abiding.

На вялікім свеце...

На вялікім свеце б'е жыццё крыніцай,
Барацьба за волю і за долю рдзее,
Маюць панаванне вера і надзея,
Асвяціць народы лепшы быт маніцца.

На вялікім свеце неба слёз не сее,
Ёрмаў не майструе крыўда-чараўніца,
Не галубіць думак цемра-асляпніца
І не водзіць душаў пагібення кнеяй.

На вялікім свеце б'юць званы на славу,
Людзі з плеч скідаюць ланцуговы скруты,
К сонцу йдуць браточна з рабскае пакуты.

На вялікім свеце ўсё ідзе па праву,
Па законе Божым, з яснатой яскравай...
А у нас, у нас што?.. Толькі звоняць путы...

1912

Out in the great world

Out in the great world, life chimes like a bubbling freshet,
The battle for bright fate and freedom blazes crimson,
Faith and hope maintain there constant their dominion,
Peoples are invited to life's more worthy session.

In the great world, heaven sows no teardrops stinging,
Injustice - that foul witch, frames no yokes of oppression,
Blinding darkness will not crush thought and expression,
Nor entice souls into traps, and to doom bring them.

Out in the great world, bells chime in all their glory,
People from their shoulders slough the cramping fetters,
From slavery's woes, they take a new path, sunward, better.

Out in the great world, all proceeds rightly, surely,
According to God's law, shining in bright glory...
But here, what do we here? Just set our chains a clatter.

Я люблю

Я люблю ўсходы нашых палеткаў,
І спавітыя ў зелень лугі,
І шум бору пануры, глухі,
І шаптанне крынічнае ўлетку...

Я люблю упрыгожану ў мхі
Нашу вёску - сваёй крыўды сведку,
Свой народ - гэту звяўшую кветку,
Цэлы край - родны мне й дарагі.

Я люблю ясны вочы і грудзі
І стан гібкі дзяўчыны-красы:
Аб ёй брэджу на яве і ў сне.

Я люблю і заву, бы ў нялюддзі,-
Чуюць кліч мой сухія лясы,
Кліч: хто ж любіць, хто любіць мяне?

1912

I love

I love the first shoots that make our fields quicken,
And the meadows swaddled in fresh green,
And the forest sounds that sadly keen,
And a summer freshet's murmured trickle...

I love our village decked with mossy sheen,
Witness to all the wrongs on it inflicted,
Our people, like a flower wilted, stricken,
Dear to me is our country's every scene.

I love the sparkling eyes and the soft breast
And the lissom form of a fair maid,
Awake, asleep, think of her constantly,

I love - and cry out in my loneliness:
And the dry forest hears the cry I've prayed,
The cry: O who, O who is there loves me?

Бацькаўшчына

З зямлёй і небам звязывае мяне ніць -
Неразарваная веквечна павуціна:
Зямля мяне галубіць, як вернага сына,
А сонца мне душу не кідае туліць.

Яшчэ ў калысцы я научыўся з песень сніць
Аб гэтых блізкіх мне, а цесных так мясцінах:
Што роднай нівы я мільённая часціна,
Што зоркі роднай ў сэрцы мне іскрынка тліць.

Так Бацькаўшчыну я здабыў сабе без злосці,
Узрос з яе й чужых з яе не скінуў косці,
Грудзьмі тулюсь к ёй, як да матчыных грудзей.

І калі здзекваецца нада мною хтосьці -
Над Бацькаўшчынай здзекваецца ён маей,
Калі ж над ёй - мяне тым крыўдзіць найцяжэй.

1915

My native land

I'm bound to earth and sky by a thread wondrous strong,
Eternal gossamer that none can break or sever,
The earth caresses me, like her true son ever,
The bright sun holds my soul in its caresses long.

Even in my cradle I learned to know from song
Of all things close to me, of my home's narrow tether:
That I am but a millionth part from my field severed,
That the stars strike the sparks that bright in my heart throng.

Thus a native land I gained without strife or anger,
I grew with her, I'll not lay my bones among strangers,
I huddle to her close, as to my mother's breast,

And if someone should threaten me with harm or danger,
The threat upon my motherland is likewise pressed,
If he threaten her, I am the more distressed.

Маё цярпенне

Маё цярпенне, мой крывавы боль -
Што значаць перад мукамі мільёнаў,
Дзе безнадзейны стогны родзяць стогны,
А слёзы грызуць вочы ўсім, як соль!

Хоць дух мой ўзносіцца пад неба столь,-
Як галавой аб мур, там б'е паклоны.
Але як мал мой гэты ўздых шалёны...
Мой крык перад малітвай свету - ноль!

I веру я, што я нішто ў быцці -
Іначай думаць не дае сумленне,-
Аднак чаму ж здаецца мне нязменне,

Што меж майму цярпенню не знайсці,
Што так вяліка мне яно ў жыцці,
Як міліёнаў разам ўсіх цярпенне!

1915

My suffering

My suffering, my pain with anguish fraught,
What does it mean while millions likewise suffer
While hopeless groan and groan again they utter,
And tears claw at the eyes of all like salt.

Although my soul aspires to heavenly vault,
And with my pleas against it ever batters,
So small my frenzied sighing - can it matter?
Faced with the whole world's prayers my cry is naught!

And I believe I am the least of creatures -
My conscience will not grant that I think other -
And yet somehow, it seems to me forever,

That this my suffering has no bound nor ceasing,
But in my life as great a sum it reaches
As all those millions suffering together.

На суд

На суд вам, кніжнікі, сябе я аддаю,
Судзіце па стаццях, як піша ваш закон;
Было ж жыццё мне - узаконены прыгон,
Хоць я не даў вам і не дам стаптаць душу сваю.

Мінаў я вашу фарысейскую сям'ю,
Мяне не збэсціў вашым ідалам паклон,
Калі ж з грудзей і вылятаў пракляцця стогн,
То кляў я сам сябе і мук сваіх змяю.

Нічым грашыць ад вас грашнейшым я не ўмеў,-
Піў чарку крыўды і цярпення - ўсё да дна,
І не спаганіла мяне аблуда ні адна.

Адзін грэх толькі лёг мне на душу, як леў,
Праступак, суддзі, мой: я сэрца, сэрца меў!
Але ці ж гэта так страшэнная віна?!

1915

To the court

To the court, o scribes, I yield myself to you,
Judge me with the statutes written in your code,
All my life in legal serfdom I abode,
Though I'd not let you crush my soul, nor will I do.

I passed by, ignored, your pharisaic crew,
I admit no homage to your idols owed,
If a groan of cursing fled my breast, its load
Was curse of self and snake of pain that gnawed me
through.

Never sinned I sin that with your sins could vie,
To the lees I drank the cup of suffering,
Yet not once did it corrupt me deep within.

Only one sin on my soul like a lion did lie,
Judge then this, my fault, a heart, a heart had I!
But, in truth can this be such a grievous sin?

Сярод магіл

Сярод магіл, на плечы ўзняўшы крыж свой, стану,
Як пасланец з магіл ад спячых там прарокаў,
І ў даль сягну, дзе толькі можа сягнуць вока,
І скрозь туды, дзе вольнай думкаю дастану.

І кліч пушчу скрозь ад кургану да кургану,
Як віхраў лёт па ўсёй бязмежнасці шырокай,
Кліч-заклінанне векавечнага зароку,
Што ў гуслях толькі дрэмле, ў песню ўчараваны.

Прадсмертнаю кляцьбой канаючага раба,
Малітвай грэшніка, зарэзаўшага матку,
Звярнуся к сонцу, сонцу без канца й пачатку.

Хай спаліць мне душу, як ствол разбіты граба,
Хай вочы высмаліць, як кветку ў лілы слабай,
Але і крыж мой спапяліць хай папарадку!

1915

Among the graves

Among the graves I stand, my cross upon my shoulder,
An envoy from the graves, words of dead prophets bearing,
And I reach to the distance, as far as eye is faring,
And everywhere that my free thought can venture boldly.

And I send forth a cry, from mound to mound unfolding,
Like whirlwinds' flight through the broad spaces tearing,
A cry, a battle-slogan from oath of age-old swearing,
That only dreams in harps, where songs enchanted hold it.

With a dying slave's last agonised death-rattle,
With the dark prayer of a mother-murdering sinner,
I seek the sun, the sun without end or beginning.

Let my soul be burned like tree-trunk felled and shattered,
Let my eyes wilt like a frail lily-flower - no matter –
Only let my cross blaze forth with fire unstinted.

Таварыш мой

Ідзе за мной услед касцісты, бледны труп,-
Як цень,- за мной, пры мне, куды я ні ступлю;
Ці я устану, ці ў пасцелі мёртва сплю -
Са мной заўсёды ён, заўсёды гэты жывы слуп.

Вакруг мяне пабудаваў жалезны зруб,
Ператварыў ў турму бязмежную зямлю,
Садраў чуццё - ці я цярплю, ці не цярплю,
Здушыў вужача грудзі ў сто сталёвых шруб.

Таварыш шчыры мой, люблю, люблю цябе!
Ні час, ні чалавеча злосць цябе не з'есць;
Ты - пасланец мой, ты - сама аб шчасці весць!

Цябе, мой труп, я ў сне і ў явы барацьбе
Не кіну, як не кінеш ты мяне ў жальбе...
О, чэсць табе, маё ты Адзіноцтва, чэсць!..

1915

My companion

Behind me a corpse paces, skeletal and pale.
Like a shadow with me, wheresoe'er I tread;
Whether I rise or lie in stupor on my bed,
A living stock, with me, it ever, ever trails.

Round me it has raised iron bars into a jail,
Turned into a prison earth's unbounded spread.
Suffer I or no - it makes all feeling dead,
Snakelike, crushed my breast with a hundred steely coils.

My faithful companion, I love you tenderly,
Not time nor human malice can gnaw thee, make thee less,
Though art my envoy, - sole, thou speakst of happiness

Whether I sleep or grapple with reality,
I'll not leave thee and thou'lt not leave my misery...
O hail to thee, all hail to thee, my loneliness!

Чаму?

Няма для духа вольнага граніцы, меры,
Дзе б ён сягнуць не смеў, дзе б ён не узлунаў;
У хаосе быцця, у цьме ўсясветных з'яў
Ён не ніштожыцца, ў сябе не губіць веры.

Яму да тайнаў душ і сэрц адкрыты дзверы,
Ўсё тое спазнае, што бег сталеццяў не спазнаў;
Як фенікс з попелаў, узносіцца з канаў,
На дно якіх яго спіхаюць цемраў зверы.

Магутны, векавечны, створан з сонц мільёнаў,-
Гром, перуны ў руках трымаць, спыняць не слаб,
Хоць бы ў агні кіпеў, ў віхрах марозаў зяб...

Аднак чаму ж ты там нішто, дух непрыгонны,
Дзе, дружна звонячы ў кайданы ўсімі тоны,
Крывёй, пажарамі частуе раба раб?

1915

Why?

For the free spirit no measure or limits bound it,
Nowhere is barred to it, whither it cannot soar,
It will not perish or lose faith in self, though roars
Life's chaos, and dark universal shapes surround it.

It opens doors to hearts', souls' mysteries profoundest,
It learns what was not learned in the long years of yore,
Like phoenix from the ashes, it will rise once more
From the pit where beasts of darkness would confound it.

Mighty, eternal, from a million suns created,
Thunder and lightning in its hands, it will not fail,
Though the fire seethes it, though the frosty tempests flail...

Why do you count for naught, here, spirit of unabated
Strength, here where, their fetters chiming o'er their fate, a
Slave gives his fellow slave blood and fire in full scale.

Для Бацькаўшчыны

Я зноў заснуўшую было жалейку
Бяру і пробую ў ёй галасоў:
Ці хопіць светлых, звонкіх думак-слоў,
Ці гладка пойдзе песня-дабрадзейка?

І пачынаю йграць з трывогай нейкай,
Хоць песня як і з даўных б'е часоў,-
Звініць, як вецер паміж верасоў,
І ўперагонкі рвецца з салавейкай.

А ўсё ж як тамка сваякі-суседзі
Яе паймуць, хацелася бы знаць,-
Ці блаславяць, ці ўтопчуць гідка ў гаць?

Адно, снуючы з сумам па праследдзі,
Я голасна йграць буду ў тайным брэдзе,
Для Бацькаўшчыны-маці буду йграць!

1918

For my native land

I take my flute, so long in slumber lying,
And try once more to make its voices heard;
Will they suffice, those shining thoughts and words,
Will its benevolent song soar, smoothly flying?

And I begin to play, with some fear lying
On me, though the song as of old is stirred
Chimes like breeze through the heather, and like bird
Its trills with the sweet nightingale are vying.

And still I wonder, how my song will seem, though,
To kinsmen-neighbours? Will they bless it, say?
Or in the bog to drown cast it away?

Yet, as my path I wander, sadly dreaming,
I shall play loud 'midst nightmare's secret looming,
For native land, my mother, I shall play.

Наша гаспадарка

Спрадвеку мы у родным краю гаспадарым,-
Свае загоны сеем, пасцім статак свой;
З надзеяй сустрачаем выраі вясной,
З надзеяй ўвосень іх праводзім над папарам.

Спрадвеку ходзім пад панамі і пад царам
На недруга й на бліжняга свайго вайной,
Хоць нам за нашу кроў падзякаю адной -
Крыжы і хаты нашы скошаны пажарам!

Так гаспадарым мы і дома і за домам,
Усё ждучы пацехі з севу і жніва,
Ждучы дарма, як летам жджэ расы трава.

Чужы і свой хлеб станавіцца жорсткім комам,
І душыць кліч: ці доўга будзе нам заломам
Варшава панская і царская Масква.

1918

Our husbandry

From ancient times we've been husbandmen in our land here,
Here we sow our furrows, pasture our flocks and herds
Here in spring with hope greet the migrating birds,
With hope in autumn wave off their departing bands, here.

From ancient times beneath a lord or a tsar's hand here,
We have gone forth to wars by foe or neighbour stirred.
Though for the blood we spilt of thanks came not a word:
Only our homes and crosses to the flames were damned here.

Thus in home and field our husbandry we practice,
Hoping aye for seed and crop that nothing mars,
Vainly, as grass hopes for dew when summer chars

Bringing forth our bread and others' bread in anguish,
Choking back the cry: how long must we still languish
Neath Warsaw of the lords and Moscow of the tsars?

Пчолы

Мой сад калодамі абведзен мёдных пчол,
Што гаманяць, як неўгамонныя музыкі;
Іх з лета ў лета звоняць звончастыя зыкі
І далятаюць да блізкіх і дальніх сёл.

Я дбаю аб вуллёх - куру, свянчу наўкол,
Запасу ўвосень мёду кідаю вялікі,
Сачу зімою, каб чарвяк не ўбіўся дзікі,
Вясною шчыра падчышчаю верх і дол.

Але як дойдзе час выходзіць рою ў свет,
Ён не садзіцца, дзе назначу я пасадку,
А коціцца, чужы дзе зацвітае цвет.

Або як мёд пайду я падглядаць у кадку,
І тут бяда - не ўсё ў парадку і даглядку:
Як рой, і мёд падгледзеў ўжо сваяк-сусед.

1918

Bees

My orchard's girt with tree-stump hives of honey-bees
That sing like music-makers with unending humming,
Their bell-song bellies out from summer unto summer.
To near and distant villages it flies forth constantly.

I tend the hives, smoke them, bless them as it should be,
In autumn-time I leave a mighty store of honey,
I watch in winter lest some parasite may come in,
In springtime, top and base I cleanse devotedly.

But when the time of swarming comes around - that day
The bees decline to settle where I built their arbour,
Off where another's blossoms bloom they swiftly stray,

And when I go for honey to the vat, my labour
Is all in vain... More trouble!...By my kinsman-neighbour
Just like the swarm, the honey has been whisked away!

***

JAKUB KOLAS

Jakub Kolas (real name Kanstancin Mickievič, 1882-1956)
was born in the village of Akinčycy in the Minsk region. After
training in Niaśviž, he began teaching in 1902, but was active
in the political uprising of 1906 and accordingly imprisoned
between 1908 and 1911, where, however, he was able to
continue to write. Kolas had in fact begun writing verse at the
age of twelve, and 'Naš rodny kraj' (Our Native Land) was
published in *Naša niva* in 1906; his first collection, 'Pieśni
žurby' (Songs of Sorrow) appeared in 1910. The two works
at the centre of his reputation as a poet were both begun while
he was in prison: 'Novaja ziamlia' (The New Land, completed
1923) and 'Symon-muzyka' (Simon the Musician, completed
1925). In 1926 Kolas was awarded the title of 'People's Poet
of the Belarusian SSR', and from 1929 until his death he was
Vice-President of the Academy of Sciences.

Kolas was a dramatist, prose writer and, above all,
poet. Before turning to his verse it is worth mentioning that
his prose trilogy *Na rostaniach* (At the Crossroads, 1921-54)
has some claims to be the first Belarusian novel of depth and
substance. It was preceded by a series of humorous and socially
acute narratives, including 'Paslušnaja žonka' (An Obedient
Wife, 1909) and 'Batrak' (The Farm Labourer, 1910). Both
of his major narrative poems, particularly 'Novaja ziamlia',
may be regarded as novels in verse. They were preceded by

poems of lament written with surprising mastery of balance and conciseness of diction, such as 'Voraham' (To Our Enemies, 1906) and 'Mužyk' (The Peasant, 1909), which from an early stage (intensified by his imprisonment) often call for resistance to autocracy and exploitation. A particularly vivid verse is 'Asadzi nazad!' (Stand Back, Move Aside!, 1908), a miniature narrative poem using the title as chorus, that ends when the subject of the peremptory order, a peasant aroused beyond endurance, is finally arrested. Kolas's prison poems are rebellious rather than sorrowful, despite the title of one of the best of them, 'Sochnu marna ja ŭ astrozie...' (I Languish Miserably in Prison, 1909); all of them show keen political and national awareness. Nature lyrics came to Belarusian literature only in the early twentieth century, and Kolas quickly showed himself a master of this genre with poems like, for instance, 'Nioman' (The River Nioman, 1906) and 'Adliot žuraŭlioŭ' (Departure of the Cranes, 1909), whilst some verses like 'Chmary' (Clouds, 1907) and 'Pieśni viasny' (Songs of Spring, 1909) treat nature more allegorically, usually to illustrate social and political ideas.

'Novaja ziamlia' has sometimes been described as an encyclopedia of Belarusian life, and its opening lines have even gone beyond poetry to commerce in a chain of grocery stores called 'Rodny Kut' (Native Nook). In the first sections of this epic work the treatment of nature is restrained, though undoubtedly poetic, as it was in so many works of the *Naša niva* period; the plot is simple, and the two main characters, Michal and Antoś, from whose viewpoint events are seen, are presented with straightforward realism, rather than any psychological depth; the sympathy and enthusiasm that infuse the work lend this quest for land something of the air of a family chronicle. Vera's translation that was included in the anthology *Like Water, Like Fire* included extracts from Parts I,

II, XVI, and the whole of Part XXX. Her translation of other parts was made much later in life. We can only regret that there was not time to complete the English version of the whole of this emblematic work.

Kolas responded strongly to times of change and crisis, as in 'Da pracy' (To work, 1917) and 'Holas ziamli' (The Voice of the Land, 1941), but some of his Soviet works fall far below the standard of the great narrative poems. As a whole, however, Belarus's greatest epic poet and first major novelist remain a source of inspiration to many of the post-Stalin generation of scholars and writers, who could work in more favourable conditions than he himself had enjoyed.

Prof. Arnold McMillin
London

НОВАЯ ЗЯМЛЯ

I. ЛЕСНІКОВА ПАСАДА

(радкі 1-84)

Мой родны кут, як ты мне мілы!..
Забыць цябе не маю сілы!
Не раз, утомлены дарогай,
Жыццём вясны мае убогай,
К табе я ў думках залятаю
І там душою спачываю.
О, як бы я хацеў спачатку
Дарогу жыцця па парадку
Прайсці яшчэ раз, азірнуцца,
Сабраць з дарог каменні тыя,
Што губяць сілы маладыя, —
К вясне б маёй хацеў вярнуцца.

Вясна, вясна! не для мяне ты!
Не я, табою абагрэты,
Прыход твой радасны спаткаю, —
Цябе навек, вясна, хаваю.
Назад не прыйдзе хваля тая,
Што з быстрай рэчкай уплывае.
Не раз яна, зрабіўшысь парам,
На крыллях сонца дойдзе к хмарам
Ды йзноў дажджом на рэчку сыдзе —
Ніхто з граніц сваіх не выйдзе,
З законаў, жыццем напісаных,
Або на дол спадзе ў туманах.
Але хто нам яе пакажа?
На дол вадой ці снегам ляжа?

Не вернешся, як хваля тая,
Ка мне, вясна ты маладая!..

Вось як цяпер, перада мною
Ўстае куточак той прыгожа,
Крынічкі вузенькая ложа
І елка ў пары з хваіною,
Абняўшысь цесна над вадою,
Як маладыя ў час кахання,
Ў апошні вечар расставання.
І бачу лес я каля хаты,
Дзе колісь весела дзяўчаты
Спявалі песні дружным хорам,
З работ ідучы позна борам.
Несліся зыкі песень здольных,
Ў лясах раз-пораз адбівалісь,
І ім узгоркі адклікалісь,
І радасць біла ў песнях вольных.
А хвоі, елкі векавыя
Пад зыкі песень маладыя
Маўчком стаялі ў нейкай думе,
І ў іх ціхусенечкім шуме
Няслось вячэрняе маленне
Ўгару, святое аддаленне

Каля пасады леснiковай
Цягнуўся гожаю падковай
Стары, высокі лес цяністы.
Тут верх асіны круглалісты
Сплятаўся з хвоямі, з дубамі,
А елкі хмурымі крыжамі
Высока ў небе выдзялялісь,
Таемна з хвоямі шапталісь.

Заўсёды смутныя, бы ўдовы,
Яны найбольш адны стаялі,
І так маркотна пазіралі
Іх задуменныя галовы!
Лес наступаў і расступаўся,
Лужком зялёным разрываўся;
А дзе прыгожыя загібы
Так міла йшлі каля сядзібы,
Што проста імі б любаваўся…
А знізу гэты лес кашлаты
Меў зелянюсенькія шаты
Лазы, чаромхі ці крушыны,
Алешын ліпкіх, верабіны.
Глядзіш, бывала, і здаецца,
Што скрозь сцяну галін жывую,
Скрозь гэту тканку маладую
Ні мыш, ні пташка не праб'ецца.
Цякла тут з лесу невялічка
Травой заросшая крынічка,
Абодва берагі каторай
Лазняк, ракітнік абступалі;
Бруіліся ў цяньку іх хвалі
І ў луг чуць значнаю разорай
Ішлі спакойна між чаротаў,
Рабілі многа заваротаў,
Аж покі ў Нёман не ўцякалі.
…………………………
(радкі 195-244)
На прыгуменні, поруч з садам,
Павець з гумном стаяла радам,
А пад паветкаю прылады:
Вазок, калёсы, панарады,
Старыя сані, восі, колы

І вулляў некалькі на пчолы,
Яшчэ някончаных; судзіна,
Стары цабэрак, паўасміна
І розны хлам і лом валяўся,
Ад сонца, дожджыку хаваўся —
Патрэбны рэчы, ёсць вядома!
Гуменца, крытае саломай,
Ад доўгіх часаў пасівела;
Салома кудламі вісела,
Яе вятры параздзімалі,
А трохі хлопцы пасцягалі,
На стрэху лазячы, бывала, —
Іх гэта забаўка займала.
А пад шчытом на павуціне
Нішчымны колас-сіраціна
Ў зацішку лёгенька гайдаўся;
З якіх ён часаў там трымаўся,
То Бог яго святы ўжо знае!
Будоўля, больш яшчэ старая,
З гнілой, вагнутаю страхою
Стаяў хлявец якраз напроці
І чуць ліпеў, як бы на плоце
Гаршчок, разбіты качаргою.
Стары, паедзены чарвямі,
Набок пахілены вятрамі,
Глядзеў хлеў гэты старычынай,
Пахілай доляй жабрачынай;
А збоку, ў полі, недалёка
Стаяў прыгрэбнік адзінока,
Пахілкам, горкім сіратою,
У дол упёршыся страхою.
Ў глыбі двара стаяла хата
І выглядала зухавата

Паміж запушчанай будовы,
Як бы шляхцянка засцянкова,
Што ў дзень святы каля касцёла,
Чуць-чуць падняўшы край падола,
Так важна ходзіць з парасонам,
Спадніцай верціць, як агонам,
З дарожак пыл, пясок зганяе
І ў вочы хлопцам заглядае.
За хатай поле пачыналась,
Дзе жыта хораша гайдалась
І рос авёс, ячмень і грэчка, —
Было прытульнае гняздзечка!..

II. РАНЩА Ў НЯДЗЕЛЬКУ

(радкі 1-88)
Дзень быў святы. Яшчэ ад рання
Блінцы пякліся на сняданне,
І ўжо пры печы з чапялою
Стаяла маці... Пад рукою
Таўкліся дзеці, заміналі
Або смяяліся, спявалі.
Услон заняў сваё ўжо места,
На ім стаяла дзежка цеста,
І апалонік то і дзела
Па дзежцы боўтаў жвава, смела
І кідаў цеста ў скавародкі.
Давала піск яно кароткі,
Льючыся з шумам на патэльні,
І ў жар стаўлялася пякельны;
І там з яго ўжо ўвачавідкі
Пякліся гладзенькія пліткі
Блінцоў, спаднізу наздраватых,

Угору пышна, пухла ўзнятых,
І ўжо адтуль рукою маткі
На ўслон шпурляліся аладкі,
А дзеці іх даўно сачылі
І на ляту блінцы лавілі,
Заядла мазалі іх здорам.
Стаяў асобна ў місцы скорам
Сяго-таго для верашчакі.
Хоць невялікія прысмакі —
Цыбуля, перчык, ліст бабкоў
Ды сальца некалькі брускоў,
Мука і квас — і ўся прыправа,
Але ўсё ж снеданне цікава;
А для дзяцей найбольша свята
Абы наесціся багата.
І звон аб прыпек скавародны,
Так блізкі сэрцу, так ім родны,
У нейкім радасным настрою
Спяваў ім песняю святою
І лашчыў сэрцы іх і вушы
І поўніў радасцю ім душы,
Такі прыемны, мілагучны,
У той прыемнасці выключны,
Ён разліваўся па ўсім целе
І ўмомант іх знімаў з пасцелі.
Недарма ж дзядзька іх, бывала,
Каб пабудзіць каго з іх жвава
Пагнаць каровак ранічкою,
У прыпек біў скаварадою.
Цяпер, здаволіўшысь ядою,
Дзяцінай цешыліся гульнёю.
Хто бегаў з кіем каля хаты —
Ганяў курэй. Як парасяты,

Ў пяску капаліся сястрычкі.
Алесь хадзіў каля крынічкі,
Што з лесу тут жа выцякала
І дужкай хату агібала,
Хадзіў, свістаў пад голас птушак,
Збіраў ён ягадкі ў гарнушак.
Ўсе парасходзіліся з хаты,
І кожны дзелам быў заняты:
Міхал у лес пайшоў ранютка
Рабіць звычайныя абходы;
Антось спаць доўга не меў моды,
А як надарыцца мінутка
Часіны вольнай ці святы дзень,
Ну хоць адзін разок на тыдзень
Хадзіў на Нёман ці на тоні —
Рыбак быў дзядзька наш Антоні,
Як і работнік, адмысловы;
А Ўладзік пасвіў дзесь каровы,
Травіў чужыя сенажаці;
А дома з дзецьмі была маці.
Яе жаночая работа
І гэта вечная турбота
То каля печы, то на полі,
Сказаць, не зводзіцца ніколі.
Адно прыпыніш — там другое,
Глядзіш, як бачыш, набяжыць,
І ручак некалі злажыць —
Жыццё жаночае такое!
Так і цяпер: печ зачыніла,
Работу ў хаце прыпыніла —
Ідзі ў гарод ты па бацвінне:
Другі раз есці просяць свінні.
А гэты Юзік-шаляніца,

Малы яшчэ, зусім дурніца,
Так пад нагамі і таўчэцца
Або, як хвост той, валачэцца
І ад работы адрывае
І толькі сэрца ад'ядае.

V. ПЯРЭБАРЫ

(радкі 1-63)
Вясны чакаў Міхал з сям'ёю,
Чакаў з трывогаю: вясною
Ў лясніцтве йшла ператасоўка
Служачых нізшых, пераходы —
Тут так вялося з году ў годы, —
І як ні думае галоўка,
Нічога выдумаць не можа;
Ніяка просьба не паможа,
Калі на чым ляснічы ўпрэцца.
— А можа, дасць Бог, ператрэцца.
І тут гадок ці два пабудзем, —
Сабе не верачы і людзям,
Міхал так думаў, сумняваўся
І тут астацца спадзяваўся.

Ды раз у сесію Міхася
К сабе ляснічы заклікае.
«Ну, гэта нешта азначае», —
Ў Міхала думка праняслася.
І ў канцылярыю ўваходзіць,
Вачэй з ляснічага не зводзіць,
Чагось-та важнага чакае.
— Ага, ты тут! Ну, чалавеча,
Збірай манаткі і ў Парэчча

За добры час перабірайся!
Перад Вялікаднем старайся
Туды, на месца, перабрацца.
Жыві там, нечага баяцца.
— Панок, за што? — Міхал пытае. —
Што за прычына ёсць такая?
Ці я па службе правініўся?
Ці на мяне пан угнявіўся?
Я не прадаў, не ўкраў нічога...
Скажы, панок, на літасць Бога,
За што нас пан перамяшчае?
Ляснічы строга пазірае.
— Мне чалавек там добры трэба,
А не гультай які, нязгрэба;
Такі ляснік, як ты, каторы
Не будзе спаць п'яны ў разоры...
Парэчча — месца неблагое,
І поле там не так пустое,
Хоць менш яго, затое ж — паша!
Дык будзе хлеб табе і каша.
Пакуль я жыў, і ты не згінеш,
Свае сям'і нябось не кінеш —
Куды ты дзенешся? трымайся,
Жыві і з Богам разжывайся.
Пайшоў Міхал наш у задуме,
А па дарозе к цётцы Хруме
Ён трапіў з гора выпіць чарку,
Каб галаве яго на карку
Было лягчэй крыху трымацца.
— І што за страх перабірацца? —
Міхал дарогай разважае. —
Мяне ляснічы паважае!..
А месца, праўда, не ліхое...

«І г-э-э-эй ты, наша жыццё зло-оо-е!» —
Міхась у лесе песню цягне
І тахты стрэльбай выбівае,
Назад, наперад выкідае,
Зайсці скарэй дадому прагне
Навінай важнай падзяліцца.
Ідзе ён смела, не баіцца…

VI. КАЛЯ ЗЯМЛЯНКІ

(радкі 151-185)
Памалу, звольна і ў Парэччы
(Такая ўрода чалавеча)
Зжываліся з месцам, прывыкалі,
Гняздо старое забывалі,
І праз якіх дзве-тры нядзелі
Ўжо весялей на свет глядзелі
Будынкі гэтыя старыя —
Яны зрабіліся як не тыя.
Агледзеў іх Антось, падправіў
І шулы новыя паставіў
Ў гнілы паркан, і лом сабралі,
Ды шыбы ў вокны паўстаўлялі,
Бо не любілі непарадку,
І пачалі жыць зноў спачатку.

Ды йзноў бяда: праз год вясною
Згарэла хата з варыўнёю
І ўвесь набытак, што быў ў дому.
Пажар той выбухнуў, як з грому,
Хоць ён і меў свае прычыны.
Як на бяду, пайшлі мужчыны

І Ўладзік з імі ўрассыпную:
Адзін у лес, той да адбору,
З сахою трэці ў гэту пору
Араў дзесь пасеку старую;
Дык што магла з дзяцьмі малымі
Зрабіць жанчына адзінютка?
І ўсё згарэла дачысцютка,
Прапала марна ў чорным дыме.
Зазнала жалю гаспадыня:
Ў агні згарэла яе скрыня
З усім пасагам і набыткам;
Прапалі хусты яе, світка,
Згарэлі кросны, рад Багоў
І грошай сорак сем рублёў.
Хоць, праўда, Костусь не збаяўся
І смела з пожарам змагаўся…

VIII. СМЕРЦЬ ЛЯСНІЧАГА

(радкі 132-140)
Так смерць ляснічага старога
Міхала моцна ўскалыхнула
І ўсё ўверх дном перавярнула.
І тут у першы раз Міхала
Вось гэта думка напаткала:
Купіць зямлю, прыдбаць свой кут,
Каб з панскіх выпутацца пут,
І там зажыць сабе нанова:
Свая зямля — вось што аснова!

XI. ДЗЕДАЎ ЧОВЕН

(радкі 1-37)
Міхал вайшоў у хату злосны.
— Ах ты, вар'яце безлітосны!
За што ты лаеш? за што хаеш?
Што да мяне ты, скажы, маеш?
Чаго чапляешся слатою,
Каб ты не ведаў век спакою!
А прападзі ты, гад шалёны! —
І доўга сыпаліся праклёны,
Пакуль Міхал свой гнеў не выліў.
— Але ж і я яго зажыліў!
І зразу змоўк, сабача морда! —
Міхал прамовіў досыць горда. —
Прагоніць вон — хай праганяе,
А служба знойдзецца такая:
Мяне сам князь у замку знае!

— І маладзец, — гаворыць жонка, —
Ды трэба больш было насыпаць,
Каб аж пайшло калоць пад кіпець,
Каб ззелянеў ён, як зялёнка.
Прагнаць! за што? Украў, ці што, ты?
За лес спраўляеш сабе боты?
Ці прапіваў дабро скарбова?
Не будзе гнаць цябе за слова:
Няма прычын. А папусціся,
Тады ідзі ты хоць тапіся.

— Ото ж зараза! от халера!
От дачакалі сабе звера!
Прыпільнаваць бы дзе брыду, —
За «гітал», падлу, ды ў ваду!

63

Парваць бы ноздры качарэжкай
Або глузды адбіць даўбешкай;
I не было б табе граху:
Забіў, як вош або блыху! —
I дзядзька моцна абурыўся
I разважаць яшчэ пусціўся:
Ці быў бы грэх, ці грэх не быў,
Калі б падлоўчага забіў?

XIII. ПАДГЛЯД ПЧОЛ

(радкі 1-25)
Пакуль што досыць аб панох:
Яны прыеліся, дальбог!
Яны без сэрца і сляпыя,
I ўсе заходы іх пустыя,
I пусты іх усе імкненні
Назад ход часаў павярнуць
I дзіркі палкамі заткнуць
I перарваць жывыя звенні,
Якіх вякі не перарвалі
У гістарычным перавале.
Ім цёмна, нема кніга лёсу,
Яны не бачаць далей носу
I рубяжоў свае пасады...
Ану іх к ліху! ну іх к ляду!
Час у Парэчча зноў вярнуцца
I ў іншых хвалях скупануцца.

Парэчча — слаўная мясціна,
Куток прыгожы і вясёлы:
Як мора — лес, як неба — долы,
Зіхціць у кветках лугавіна...

А колькі ягад і парэчак!
Як пахне мёдам поле грэчак,
Калі пачнуць яны цвісці!..
Ну, як тут пчол не завясці:
Ім столькі выгад тут, прастору!

XVI. ВЕЧАРАМІ

(радкі 1-68)
Малюнкі родныя і з'явы!
Як вы мне любы, як цікавы!
Як часта мілай чарадою
Вы ўстаяце перада мною!
І так панадна смеяцеся
Жывою баграю на лесе,
І златаблескімі снапамі
Праменняў-стрэлаў над палямі,
І брыльянцістаю расою,
Калі гарачаю касою
Скрозь лісцяў сетачкі-аконцы
На ёй заззяе ціха сонца,
Яе так песціць, так кахае,
Па ёй вясёлкі рассыпае!
Я бачу роўныя пакаты
Палёў за Нёмнам і іх шаты —
Аўсоў палоскі, лавы жыта,
Што морам золата разліта;
І грэчак белыя абрусы,
І лесу два крылы, як вусы,
І цёмны роў, вадой прабіты,
Такі зацяты і сярдзіты;
Ялоўцаў шэрыя аблогі,
Дзе белы мох, сівец убогі

Пясочак жоўты засцілаюць
І дзе зайцы прыпынак маюць.
Я чую шум рознагалосы
Лясоў, лугоў, дзе звоняць косы
У часе дружнай касавіцы;
Я чую громы навальніцы,
І шум глухі буйных дажджоў,
І песні звонкія палёў,
І ціхі плач ускрай магілы.
Даўно заціх іх голас мілы,
Даўно ўсё змоўкла і прапала,
Іх толькі памяць захавала.

Але нявіднымі ніцямі
Я моцна-моцна звязан з вамі,
Малюнкі роднае краіны!
Эх, зараслі вы, пуцявіны
У гэты мілы мой куточак,
Дзе ные жоўценькі пясочак
Пад летнім сонцам, пад спякотай
І ззяе смутнай пазалотай
Над самым Нёмнам срэбраводным,
Так сэрцу блізкім-блізкім, родным.
І зараслі не палынамі,
Не крапівой, не драсянамі,
Не чаратом, не лебядою —
А беларускаю бядою.
Ды покі будзе сэрца біцца,
Яно не зможа пагадзіцца
Ні з гэтым гвалтам, ні з бядою
Над нашай роднаю зямлёю...

Эх, мілы край адвечнай мукі!

66

Пракляты будзьце, вусны, рукі,
Што на цябе ланцуг кавалі
І ў твар зняважліва плявалі!
Няхай агонь і жар пакуты
Навекі спаліць здзек той люты,
Які спрадвеку там пануе,
Над тым, хто родны скарб шануе
І хто ўсім сэрцам і душою
Астацца хоча сам сабою.
Жыві ж, наш край! Няхай надзея
Гарыць у сэрцы і мацнее,
Што хоць не мы, дык нашы дзеці
Убачаць цэльным цябе ў свеце!

XVII. ВОЎК

(радкі 78-97)
Міхал ідзе ў свае абходы,
А холад зімняе пагоды
Яго рухавіць і малодзіць,
І колькі тут разоў ён ходзіць!
Тут кожна сцежка і дарожка
Яму даўно-даўно знаёма,
Міхал у лесе, як бы дома:
Дзе ні ступала яго ножка!
Якіх куточкаў тут не знае!
Міхал ідзе, сляды чытае!
Вось тут танюткі ланцужок
Лёг так прыгожа на сняжок —
То пара кропак, то дзве рыскі,
Відаць, што мышкіны распіскі.
Другі малюнак, след — трайчаткі
Па лесе кідаюць зайчаткі;

А ліс-хітрэц, выжыга чуткі,
Па снезе цягне шнур раўнюткі:
Слядок з слядочкам супадае,
Бы лапка тут адна ступае.

(радкі 223–319)
Міхал раптоўна садрыгнуўся,
Зірнуў за Нёман і прыгнуўся,
З-за хвойкі хціва выглядае
І дубальтоўку з плеч знімае,
Увесь хвалюецца, дрыжыць:
Ваўчуга з сёл сюды бяжыць
І проста валіць на Міхала!
Аж сэрца ў радасці ўзыграла:
«Пастой жа, брат, пастой, ваўчуга!
Ужо ж спаткаю, валацуга!»
А воўк імчыцца, снег здзірае,
І толькі хвост яго мільгае,
Відаць, далі яму дзесь жаху.
«Ну, брат Міхась, не дай жа маху!»
Ён брамкі ў стрэльбе адчыняе,
Прыклад падносіць да пляча;
«Не так дасі ты стракача!» —
Міхал паціху разважае.
А воўк ляціць. Вось ён на Нёмне...
Вось ён за горкай... не відаць —
Ён будзе тут хвілін праз пяць...
«Трымайся ж, браце, цэлься, помні!»
Міхал замёр, не моргне вока:
Развязка скора, недалёка —
Вось-вось пакажацца звяруга!..
Ды доўга гэта штось натуга —
Няма, а быць ужо пара.

Цьфу ты! Што ж гэта за мара?
Ўстае Міхал, глядзіць вакола,
Як бы што страціў, невясёла,
А рукі ўсё яшчэ дрыжаць.
Ну, хоць бы, гада, напужаць!
І дзе ён дзеўся? дзе, пракляты?
Міхала рух бярэ заўзяты,
Не возьме тропу ён ніяк,
Бяжыць управа наўскасяк:
А можа, там яго спаткае,
А не, дык снег хоць запытае.
Але й туды прабег дарма:
Там слядоў яго няма.
Бяжыць назад — няма! — прапала!..
Аж нейкі пот праняў Міхала.
Міхал на Нёман тут рвануўся
І, як зірнуў, аж здрыгануўся,
І ўсё ў ім раптам задрыжала,
Аж нават шапка чуць не спала,
Калі прычын Міхал дазнаўся:
У стрыжаню воўк шалпатаўся!
Міхала згледзеў — лясь зубамі!
І злосна бліскае вачамі.

Міхал хватае дубальтоўку
І хоча выстраліць у воўка.
А потым стрэльбу апускае
І воўка зблізку разглядае.
А ён — вось тут, бяры рукамі,
Завіс на лапах, як у яме;
Стрыжэнь глыбокі, лёд пакаты,
А бедны воўк, вадой падцяты,
Скрабе па лёдзе кіпцюрамі

І носам рые, як зубамі,
І ўвесь пружыніцца і рвецца,
Але нічога не ўдаецца,
І ўсё слабее ў воўка сіла.
Ды страшна смерць, усім жыць міла!
Ён рэшту сіл ізноў збірае,
Мацней на лапы налягае,
Ды іх няма за што зацяць,
Яны слабеюць, слізгацяць
І толькі скробаюць па лёдзе,
Перабіраюць край стрыжэню,
Няма надзеі нават цену
У той яго бядзе-прыгодзе, —
Няма, ваўчок, табе збавення!
Дарэмны ўсе твае імкненні!
І ненадоўга сілы стане
Вясці з вадою тут змаганне.
Слабее воўк і абмярзае,
А плынь усё больш падбірае,
І, барукаючысь з вадою,
Ён павярнуўся галавою
І ўскінуў погляд на Міхала.
Вачамі злосна ўжо не косіць,
Глядзіць, як бы ратунку просіць...
Цьфу ты! аж шкода яго стала —
Так вочы жаласна глядзяць,
Ну, вось, дальбог, шкада страляць!

Яшчэ раз бедны воўк рвануўся,
На спіну раптам павярнуўся,
Завыў жалобна і каротка
І — шуг пад лёд той, як калодка!
І знікла ўсё: жыццё, змаганне,

І прагавітасць палявання.
Міхал стаіць і разважае,
А потым голаву ўскідае,
Як бы ён хоча запытаць,
Хоць тут нікога не відаць:
«Ну, што ты скажаш, брат, на гэта?»

XX. КАЛЯДЫ

(радкі 1-26)
Прыйшлі піліпаўкі, Мікола,
Дзянькі праходзяць больш вясёла,
Бо хоць зіма і крэпіць дужа,
І хоць бушуе яе сцюжа,
Бы тое дзікае ігрышча,
І вецер жудасна засвішча,
Як на дудзе ці на кларнеце
На нейкім злыдневым банкеце, —
Ды ўсё ж святлеюць даляў вочкі
І іх бялюткія сарочкі.
Ёсць хараство і ў гэтых зімах
І ў мёртва-белых тых кілімах,
Што віснуць-ззяюць хрусталямі
Над занямелымі лясамі,
Калі ў агністым мароз троне,
Ў крывава-багравай заслоне
Над светам рукі ціха ўздыме
І зачаруе, ўсё абніме;
А як усходзіцца завея,
І вецер з снегам задурэ,
Ды затрасецца віхрам белым!..
Эх, колькі волі ў руху смелым!
— Гуляй, зіма, твая часіна!

Ды скора будзе палавіна,
А там цяплом табе павее;
А ўдзень і сонейка прыгрэе!

XXIV. ВЯЛІКДЗЕНЬ

(радкі 82-120)

Над ціхай талаю зямлёю
Навісла ночка той парою.
Было спакойна і лагодна,
Як бы сама прырода тая
Паважнасць свята адчувае,
З людзьмі жыве супольна, згодна.
Маўчаць хваіны, ані зыку,
Не шэпне гэты бор-музыка,
Стаіць маўчком і разважае,
Відаць, Вялікадня чакае.
«Цяпер і страхі пазнікалі!»
На вуха Костусю шапталі
Якіясь думкі-весялушкі:
«Звяры Вялікдзень чуюць, птушкі,
І хвоі гэтыя, і елі,
Ліхія людзі падабрэлі,
Бо святам божым усюды вее;
З нажом разбойнік не пасмее
Залегчы ў лесе срэдзь дарогі,
Бо і заможны і ўбогі
Святы Вялікаднік святкуюць
І радасць у сэрцы сваім чуюць».
І гэту згоднасць, радасць свята
Ва ўсім Кастусік адчувае:
І ў тым, як з дзядзькам размаўляе,

На возе седзячы з ім, тата,
Чуваць яна ў пытанні брата,
І ў гэтым лесе безгалосным,
І ў мерным клыгату калёсным;
Вось так і чуеш, што й дарога
Цяпер паслушна волі Бога,
І пераказваюць навіны
Калёсам гучна каляіны.
Дарога з лесу выйшла ў поле,
Калёсы коцяцца паволі,
Шуршыць пясочак мнагазначна.
Ў сяле на цэркві чуць абачна
Блішчыць ліхтарык і мігае,
Дарожных погляд прыцягае.

XXX. СМЕРЦЬ МІХАЛА

(радкі 1-79)
Канец... Як проста гэта слова
І мнагазначна, заўжды нова!
Як часта мы пад крыжам мукі
Ў тамленні духу ўзносім рукі
І вочы, поўныя гарэння,
І прагнем мігу вызвалення!
Шчаслівы міг, бо палі путы!
Канец — і нейкі круг замкнуты
У небыццё ідзе і гіне,
Каб месца іншай даць часіне;
І вера ў той канец няўхільны
Знішчае тлен гнілы, магільны.

Канец!.. Як многа разважання
І засмучонага пытання

У гэтым простым, страшным слове
Пры іншым з'явішчы і ўмове,
Калі астатняю мяжою
Канец кладзецца між табою
І тым, што дорага і міла,
Што душу грэла і хіліла
І сэрца моцна парывала,
Як гімн у вуснах перавала,
Калі змутнелаю вадою,
Дзе сонца цешыцца сабою,
Шуміць ён вольны і імкненны
І гучна-звонны й бела-пенны!
І ты, маё апавяданне,
Жыцця адбітак, разважання,
Нязжыты след прасцяцкай долі,
Адвечны водгук праўды, волі,
Ўжо бачыш дзень свайго змяркання.
І сціхне ліры звон тужлівы,
Бо блізак захад той маўклівы,
Апошні крок твайго блукання.
І смутна мне: я жыў з табою
Адною думкаю, душою,
Насіў цябе, як носіць маці
Няясны воблік той дзіцяці.
Ды ты, відаць, не ў міг шчаслівы
На свет радзілася бурліва
Яшчэ далёкаю вясною
За мураванаю сцяною
Ў няволі жудаснай астрога,
Калі над намі ноч-аблога
Навісла цемраю густою
І гнула цяжкаю пятою,
Як неадхільная навала,

Усё, што жыцце асвятляла.
Ды ноч мінулася памалу
Ў агульным жыцця перавалу,
А там дарога, зноў дарога,
Разлука з краем і трывога
І паднявольнае блуканне
І гэта нуднае змаганне
За інтарэсы жывата,
Ды зноў варожая пята...

Як часта я жывіў табою
Ў разлуцы з роднаю зямлёю
Гадзіну смутку, летуцення
І момант радасці — натхнення!
Святым агнём душа палала,
І злучнасць-згоду адчувала
Таемных чараў-сугалосся
І чула шум тады калоссяў
На родных гонях на далёкіх
І песні жнеек яснавокіх.
А выгляд горак крутабокіх,
Лясочкаў, хвоек кучаравых,
Такіх прыветных і ласкавых,
Як дабрадушныя бабулі,
І грэлі сэрца і гарнулі,
Ў вачах стаялі, як жывыя.
Дрыжалі струны гаваркія,
Ў агульны тон суладдзя гралі
І на нявідныя скрыжалі
Трох неажыццеўленых слоў
Пісалі напісы вякоў...
Дык так: часіна развітання,

Апошні крок твайго блукання!

....

(радкі 223-260
Адзін Міхал і грэў імкненне
Давесці справу да сканчэння.
Але няўзнакі, неўзаметкі
Вязала ліха свае сеткі,
Каб іх накінуць на Міхала,
І нінавошта не зважала,
Бы тая злосная намова:
Міхал прыцяміў выпадкова
Густы, чырвоны след крываўкі!
«Эге, брат, дрэнныя праяўкі:
Прыйшла згінота на Міхася!» —
Падумаў ён у нейкім страсе,
І нават сэрца ў ім апала.
Што за праява напаткала?
Няўжо яна, смерць, неўзірана?
Не, не! аб ёй і думаць рана.
Міхал жахнуўся. Нейкі смутак,
Ліхіх пачуццяў цёмны скрутак
Яго агортваюць істоту;
Ён чуе ў свеце адзіноту,
Як бы варожых лёсаў сіла
У вочы глянула няміла
І ўстала нейкім грозным валам
Між тым жыццём і ім, Міхалам.
І першы раз ён так балюча
Адчуў той момант немінучы,
Які ўсіх нас вартуе пільна,
Бо гэта смерць — зло неадхільна.
«Няўжо памру і стану трупам,

Згнію ў зямлі нікчэмным струпам
На целе гэтае зямлі?»
І цені страшныя ляглі
Яму на душу і на сэрца,
І ён так ясна, бы ў люстэрцы,
Убачыў смерці ўсе пячаці
І ўсе адзначныя пастаці.
Міхал пачуў, што ён — пылінка,
А век людскі — адна хвілінка.

....

(радкі 314-333)
Праз нейкі час, ужо пад зіму,
Міхал у моцным быў абніму
Хваробы цяжкай і паганай,
Неспадзяванай, негаданай.
І гора ў тым: хвароба гэта
Даўно цягнулася, не з лета,
І ў тым была яе і сіла,
Што незаметна налучыла,
І спатайка гадоў праз колькі
Яе жывілі манаполькі,
Пакуль яна не разнялася
І не зваліла з ног Міхася.
Спярша Міхал перамагаўся
І той хваробе не даваўся,
А потым кінуўся і ў лекі,
Больш з саматужнае аптэкі:
Піў зёлкі розныя і травы,
Ды не палепшваў свае справы.
Да дактароў ужо па часе
Вазілі хворага Міхася.

....

(радкі 567-637)
Міхал крычыць і б'ецца ў страсе.
Заслона чуць-чуць адышлася,
Ён вочы цяжка размыкае —
Ў руцэ рука чыясь другая,
І вочы, поўныя пакуты,
Да мутных воч яго прыкуты.
Зняможан цяжкім ён змаганнем.
З глыбокім жалем, садрыганнем
Ратунку просіць у людзей,
У брата, жонкі і дзяцей,
Бо неба жорстка, неба глуха
І не прыклоніць свайго вуха,
Хоць ты прасі, хоць ты малі,
Хоць грудзі рві і сэрца вымі —
Ты не кранеш яго цвярдыні,
Яно далёка ад зямлі,
Яно зацята, бо нямое,
Яно маўкліва, бо пустое.
— Ты пазнаеш мяне, Міхаська? —
Ён уздымае вочы цяжка,
Глядзіць на жонку. — Ганна... Маці...
Ратунку дайце мне!.. О, браце!
Ратуй мяне! ратуйце, дзеткі!.. —
Сляза-палын балюча-едкі
На ўпалых вочах выступае...
Міхал зяхае — заціхае...
— Ой, свечку, свечку: ён канае!
На твары след пякельнай мукі,
На грудзі палі яго рукі.
Міхал яшчэ раз здрыгануўся,
Зяхнуў так цяжка, ўвесь памкнуўся,

78

Яшчэ раз вочы расчыняе,
Глядзіць, бы штось прыпамінае;
Ён цяжка дыша, духу мала, —
І ўсё адразу ясна стала.
— Антоська!.. родны мой! канаю...
Перагарэў, адстаў, знікаю...
Вядзі ж ты рэй, вядзі... адзін...
Як лепшы брат, як родны сын.
Бог не судзіў мне бачыць волі
І кідаць зерні ў свае ролі...
Зямля... зямля... туды, туды, брат,
Будуй яе... ты дай ёй выгляд...
На новы лад, каб жыць нанова...
Не кідай іх... Га-а-х! — І — гатова!
Ні слоў жывых, ні сэрца стуку,
І халаднеючую руку
Антось цалуе і рыдае
І к трупу з енкам прыпадае.

У полі, полі
Пры дарожачцы
Пахіліўся крыж
Над магілаю.

Беглі сцежачкі
Ў свет шырокенькі,
Прывялі ж яны
К той магіланцы!..

Ой вы, дарожанькі людскія,
Пуцінкі вузкія, крывыя!
Вы следам цьмяным снуяцеся
І ўсё блукаеце, бы ў лесе,

79

Вас горне шлях прасторнай плыні
І далягляд ружова-сіні,
Дзе так панадна свеціць сонца,
Дзе думка тчэ свае красёнцы,
Каб новы свет жыцця саткаць,
Заспакаенне сэрцу даць
І разагнаць яго трывогі!..
Прасторны шлях! калі ж, калі
Ты закрасуеш на зямлі
І злучыш нашы ўсе дарогі?

1911--1923

THE NEW LAND

I. THE FOREST WARDEN'S HOMESTEAD

(lines 1- 84)
My native nook, dear land that bred me!..
I have no power to forget thee!
Often when, from the roadway weary,
From my life's springtime, poor and dreary,
To thee on wings of thought I hasten,
And my poor soul finds rest and grace then.
O how I long, from the beginning
To tread again my road of living,
Step by step the whole path trace over,
And from the road those stones to gather,
On which young force and strength were wasted –
Back to that spring I'd wend my paces.

O Spring, O Spring, thou art not for me,
I shall not go, with thee to warm me,
To greet thy coming, joyful, merry,
Thou, Spring, I must forever bury.
For that wave will return here never
Which rolled away on the swift river,
But, into vapour oft transmuted,
Cloudward it soars on sunshine plumage,
Then, back as rain, falls to the river,
(For no one can escape, no, never,
The laws which life for him writes valid)
Or lies as mist on dale and valley;
But who is it that thinks to show where
Lies it as water or as snow there?

And thou, like wave upon the river,
Young spring, wilt come back to me never…

And now, again, before me rises
That nook in all its lovelinesses.
The curving stream-bed of the freshet,
The spruce tree and the pine that ever
Above the stream embrace together,
Like young folk in their love's devotion,
The last eve before separation.
I see the woods around the homestead,
Where once girls gaily, in the gloaming,
Sang their songs in a lovely chorus,
Late from work passing by the forest.
Notes of their fluent songs, far-trilling,
Once again by the woods were mirrored,
And with them all the hills resounded,
Forth in free billows, gladness bounded,
And firs and spruces sempiternal.
Beneath those song-notes, young and vernal,
Stood silent in some meditation,
And in their quiet murmuration
Were born the prayers of evening whispered,
Aloft, high into holy distance.

About the forest-warden's steading,
Like a lovely horse-shoe spreading,
Old and high, a forest briared,
There the round-leafed aspens' spires,
With firs and oak-trees interlacing,
Spruces their cloudy crosses tracing
High in the heavens clear, mysterious
Words to the pine-trees softly whispered,

And, like widows, ever sadly,
They in loneliness would stand there,
And so mournful was the gazing
Of their heads, aye meditating!
Now retreating, now advancing,
The woods the green meadow parted,
Here and there curves lovely wandered,
Round the homestead in fair meanders,
That one must stand there and admire them…
Below, this shaggy wood's arrayed in
Pavilions of rich green brocading –
Willow, bird-cherry, buckthorn showing,
Clinging alders too, and rowan.
And where'er your gaze is bent there,
It seems, this living wall of branches,
This young tapestry gives no chance for
Mouse or bird to leave or enter,
And here, out from the wood, a little
Spring, overgrown with grasses trickled,
And on both banks, in clusters growing,
Rose broom bushes, clumps of willow.
And in their shadow, the stream's billows
In a tiny channel flowed out
To the meadow through the rush,
Through many a meander gushing
Until they poured into the Nioman…

(lines 195-244)
 By the orchard, in the farmyard,
There a lean-to and a barn stood,
Under the lean-to were gathered
Tools and harness, cart and waggon.
Wheels and axles, old sledge-runners,

Skeps for bees – quite few in number –
Still unfinished, sundry vessels,
Old tubs, a half-bushel measure,
And all kinds of trash and lumber,
Sheltered from the rain and sun there –
For, of course, it *could* be needed.
The barn, thatched with straw, had faded
Into grey with long years passing,
Tufts of straw where winds had tossed them
Dangled from it, wild, dishevelled;
Somewhat, too, by boys bedevilled,
On the thatched roof climbing, crawling,
(That, they found, a game enthralling!)
And 'neath the gable, in a cobweb,
An orphan ear of grain was bobbing,
In the stillness, very quietly –
Truly, only God almighty
Knew how long it had kept hold there.
Another building, even older,
With roof warped and rotted dire,
Stood across the yard – a byre,
Hardly in one piece, as it were
On fence-post propped to dry, a pitcher,
Cracked by the poker. Old, worm-eaten,
By the winds battered into leaning,
It seemed like some old soul grown senile,
From beggar's fortune bent and leaning.
To one side, in the field, quite handy,
Was a wretched cold-house standing,
Like grief-bitter orphan bending,
With roof into the earth descending.
Within the courtyard, the house loomed there,
Looking smart and nicely groomed there

Beside the rest, ramshackle, faded,
Like a yeoman-peasant maiden,
On feast-days, by the Catholic chapel,
Holding her skirts up a little,
With her umbrella walking grandly,
Trailing a tail of skirts, the sandy
Dust from the path behind her sweeping,
And in the lads' eyes coyly peeping.

Beyond the house, the home-field started,
Where graceful swaying rye was planted,
Oats, barley, buckwheat and the rest there…
It was a very cosy nest there…

II. SUNDAY MORNING

(lines 1-88)
A holy day! From early dawning,
Pancakes for breakfast baked that morning,
Already by the stove with oven-
Prong in her hand, there stood the mother…
Round her the children scampered, peering,
Laughing and singing, interfering.
In its place stood the working table,
With kneading-trough and dough; the ladle
Was there at work, rapidly going
Into the kneading-trough and throwing
The dough out quickly on the griddle.
The batter gave a rapid sizzle,
Noisily flowed the griddle over,
Then into the hell-heat of the oven;
And, in the twinkle of an eye-lid,

Out from it, ready, baked like tiles, came
Pancakes, underneath all waffled,
And rising up with splendid puffing,
And, straight away, from mother's hand came
Tossed on the work-bench, these fine pancakes.
And long the children watched them, vying
To catch the pancakes in their flying,
And spread them keenly with good dripping.
The chopped meat stood there in the kitchen
Bowl, and the things to give a savour
Of sauce –'twas no exotic flavour –
Onion, pepper and bayleaf, taken
With a few slices of good bacon,
Flour and *kvass*, nothing more, but never-
The-less, breakfast excites one ever.
For children, the best feast-day party
Is when they can eat well and hearty,
The griddle on the stove-ledge chinking,
So near, so dear to them this clinking,
With such a joyful humour ringing,
It sang to them its holy singing,
Their hearts and ears sweetly caressing,
Filled souls with joy beyond expressing.
So pleasantly, so sweetly sounding,
Unique in pleasantness abounding,
Filled all their bodies to the limit,
Fetched them from bed in half-a-minute.
Not in vain then as Uncle's habit;
When he must rouse them, swift and rapid,
To drive the cows out, he was given
To chink the griddle in the oven.
Now, having stuffed themselves with eating,
They turned to childhood's games, repletely.

One with a stick went chasing quickly
Around the house, scaring the chickens.
Sisters, like little piglets rolling,
Romped in the sand. Alieś went strolling
Beside the spring, that here came flowing,
Out of the forest, its curve going
About the homestead; whistling merry
To charm the birds, and picking berries
Into a jug. Each went off easy
His own way, at his own task busy.
Michal to the wood went early, in it
To make his rounds, his usual custom;
Antoś was unused to lengthy slumber,
And when he could find a spare minute,
Some free time on a holiday he,
At least once weekly, went off gaily,
To plumb the Nioman's depths his wish – he,
Our Anton was an avid fisher,
He was an expert, a real craftsman,
Uladzik took out the cows to pasture,
(Poaching the meadows of another);
And at home, with the children, mother
About her housewife's labours fussing,
About eternal labours bustled,
Now in the field, now at the stove, a
Toil, you would say, that's never over.
This done, on *that* she is beginning,
Never a moment comes that in it
She's time to fold her hands a minute –
That is the life, alas, of women!
So now, at last, she closed the oven,
But now the household work was over,
Off to the garden, beets she's needing,

The pigs require another feeding.
And Juzik, too, the little fellow,
Still small and silly, tried to follow,
Always beneath your feet you'll find him,
Or, dragging like a tail behind you,
Ever distracts you with his needing,
And sets the heart within you bleeding.
....

V. MOVING

(lines 1-63)
Michal and family awaited
The springtime with some trepidation;
In forestry, spring meant reshuffle
Of jobs, transfers to new positions -
Year after year rolled this tradition -
However your poor head you puzzle,
You'll not think up a way to change it.
No pleas will soften the Chief Ranger
Once he decides some plan or other.
'Maybe, please God, it will blow over,
And still a year or two he'll leave us
Here!' Michal thought, without believing
Himself or others. Doubts now claimed him.
Yet still he hoped they might remain here.

Then from the Ranger came a summons
To Michal – he must interview him.
"Well, this must portend something, truly!"
The thought through Michal's head was humming.
So to the office Michal hurried,
With eyes fixed on the Ranger, worried,

He waited his instructions duly.
"Aha, you're here! Well, my man, get your
Bags packed. You're moving to Parečča!
And don't take too long! At the least you
Ought to be moved there before Easter.
Get yourself settled with your gear there,
And live there! There's no cause to fear there"!
'Why, Sir? What for?' Michal entreats him
'What have I done, Sir? What's the reason?
Have I displeased you, Sir? Or fallen
Down on my duties? I've not stolen,
Nor sold things off without permission!
For God's sake, Sir, why this decision?'
What have I done that you must move me?'
The Ranger eyes him, disapproving.
'I need a man sound and well-tried there.
No clumsy oaf nor lazy idler,
A forester like you, no toper
Lying around in drunken stupor…
Parečča's no bad post, I'll warrant.
The field, you'll find, is no way barren,
Smaller, it's true, but such good ploughland!
You'll have your bread and groats abounding.
So, while I live and you keep breathing
Your family'll have no cause for grieving.
What can go wrong? Pluck up, man! Muster
Your spirits, and, with God's help, prosper!'
Off went Michal, pondering, gloomy,
And on his way at Auntie Chruma's
Dropped in - a dram to drown his sorrows,
So that his head, relieved from worries
Might sit more lightly on his shoulders.
'Well, what's to fear in moving?' boldly

Michal now thought as home he wended.
'The Ranger praised me, seemed quite friendly.
And the posting's not bad, surely…'

'He—ey-ho, our life goes ever poo-oor-ly!'
Through the trees Michal drawls his singing,
Thumping his gun-butt to the rhythm,
Behind, before; now he feels driven
To hurry homeward, and to bring them
The mighty news of their departure,
Fearlessly now he goes, stouthearted…
…………………………………………

VI. NEAR THE MUD HUT

(lines 151- 185)
…But slowly, slowly in Parečča
(Such is the way of human nature)
They grew used to the new spot and
Their former nest was now forgotten.
When two or three weeks had passed merely,
They looked upon the world more cheerly,
And all the old buildings round them.
Were no more the state they'd found them.
Everything Antoś had inspected
And put right, new post he'd erected
In the fences' rot, the flinders
And trash were gone, he'd glazed the windows,
For they could not abide disorder,
So they began their life once more there.

Next spring, though, more grief came to smite them
The house burned down, and the barn likewise,

And all their goods in the house. Sudden
The fire exploded as if thunder,
Though it had reasons for its coming.
And what was worse, no men were home then.
Nor Uladzik, in diverse ways wending,
One to the forest, one the...... [*see note, p.* 110]
One with a plough was turning over
An old bee-field somewhere or other.
Alone, what could a woman do then
Left with small children. It all perished,
Everything that they had cherished.
In black smoke gone to rack and ruin.
Such bitterness our housewife tasted,
In flames her wedding-chest was wasted,
Her dower and household goods the fire
Took, shawls and Sunday-best attire,
The loom burned, icons in a row,
And forty-seven in cash, also.
Kastuś, though, showed no trepidation,
Boldly strove with the conflagration...

VIII. THE DEATH OF THE OLD RANGER

(lines 132-140)
...And so the death of the old Ranger
Shook Michal mightily, unnerved him.
Everything was turned topsy-turvy.
In Michal's thinking had arisen
To buy some land, have one's own nook,
And so break free from the lord's hook,
And build his life over again then...
One's own land. Yes, that is the main thing!

91

XI. GRANDFATHER'S BOAT

(lines 1-37)

Into the house Michal went, fuming,
'You heartless wretch, you raging loony!
Why d'you abuse me and ill-use me?
What have you in for me, accusing
And swearing at me, never-ceasing!…
May you not know a moment's peace, then!
Vanish like a crazed serpent, dying!'
On and on came the curses flying.
Till Michal's anger drained, abated.
'I bested him at any rate, though!
He shut up, quick, the dog-faced villain!'
Said Michal, and pride swelled within him!
'He'll oust me, will he? Well, just let him!
I'll find another job, much better.
The Duke knows of me! Sure, I'll get one!'

'Good for you!', says his wife. 'However,
You should have pressed him a bit tighter,
And stuck your claws into the blighter,
So that he'd go grass-green all over!
Oust you? Why? Have you been stealing?
You bought your boots by secret dealing
In timber? Drank away the storehouse?
For a word he'd not oust you, surely
There is now cause! But if it maybe
Happens, then go, drown yourself straightway!'
Or shove a poker up his nostril,
Or beat his brains out with a pestle!
For surely it's no sin or evil
Like lice or fleas to kill the devil!'

And Uncle's anger rose, berating,
And on he went, deliberating
Was it or was it not a sin
To do the Under-Ranger in?
………………………………….

XIII. BEEKEEPING

(lines 1-25)
Enough of chatter about lords.
Dear God, they make me sick and bored!
For blind they are, and heartless ever,
Empty and vain are their endeavours,
Empty and vain is all their striving.
To reverse the course of time,
In every hole to prod and pry,
And break apart and sunder living
Links which the long years by the hundred
On history's watershed could not sunder.
Dim they are. Fate no book exposes
To them. They can't see past their noses,
Nor past the bounds of their broad acres…
Away with them! The devil take them!
Back to Parečča let us turn now;
To swim in other waves I yearn now.

Parečča – a place truly glorious,
A nook so lovely and so joyous,
Oceans of forests, vales like heaven,
The meadows with bright blossoms riven,
What wealth of berried fruits it yields,
What scent of honey from the fields,
When the buckwheat is in flower...

93

So get some bees. This is the hour….
They've all they need here: space a-plenty…

XVI. EVENINGS

(lines 1-68)
Native pictures, scenes that call me,
How dear you are, how enthrall me,
How often, in well-loved succession
You rise before me in procession!
And so attractively come smiling,
With living porphyry beguiling
Across the woods, with sheaves gold-gleaming
Of arrow-rays on ploughland steaming,
And with diamantine dewdrops
When, its burning ray far-strewing,
Through the foliage net-window,
Quietly on it the sun glints so.
And caresses it and loves it,
Spreading rainbows bright above it.
I see level lands, far over
Nioman water, and their clothing,
Oats in strips and rye in bands there,
That like sea of gold expands there,
Buckwheat tablecloths whitely gleaming,
And two wings of forest, seeming
Like moustaches, the dark gulley
Pierced with water, harsh and stubborn,
Terraced junipers grisaille, where
White moss and poor lichen fraily
Spread above the yellow dunes there
Where the timid hares find refuge.
I hear the multi-chorused singing

Of woods and meadows with scythes ringing,
In harmonious haymaking.
I hear tempest thunders shaking,
The dull noise of abundant rain,
The chiming song of fields of grain,
And, by a graveside, quiet weeping.
Long now that voice is silence keeping,
Long now these all have gone for ever,
With only memory as their cover.

Yet still invisible threads viewless
Strongly-strongly bind me to you,
Pictures of my dear country, ever!
Ah, pathways, you are all grown over,
That once to my dear nook were leading,
Whence the yellow sands are keeping,
Under the summer sun the blinding
Heatwave and, the sad gilding shining
Over the silver-flooded Nioman,
So near the heart, so much one's own there.
Not with wormwood are you beset so,
Not with aloes, not with nettles,
Not with rushes, nor with weeds grown –
With Byelorussian grief and need grown.
But while heart beats with life's pulsation,
It knows no reconciliation,
With violence or woe that plunders
And tramples down our native country.

Dear land of torments sempiternal,
May lips and hands be cursed eternal,
Hands that have forged thy chains, exulting,
Lips that spat in thy face, insulting.

Let fire and heat with anguish flaming,
Burn out for age this insult shaming
That from past years holds lordship over
Those who their native treasure honour,
And who with heart and soul are straining
To be their own true self remaining.
Live on, my land, let hopeful longing
Burn in the heart forever stronger,
If not we, our sons' generation,
Shall see thee stand, entire, a nation.

XVII. THE WOLF

(lines 78-97)
Michal goes on his rounds as ever,
The coldness of the winter weather
Makes him move, once more young and limber,
He has gone so, times without number!
Here every path and track half-hidden
Long since within his knowledge flourished,
He is at home here in the forest:
Where is a spot he has not trodden?
Where is some unknown nook or corner?
Michal goes, reads the tracks before him!
See here, a delicate thin chain
Daintily on the snow has lain,
Two dots, and then two lines appearing,
A mouse's signature, quite clearly.
A second picture; a track triple
That through the wood some hares have stippled;
And master fox, know-all, sharp-witted,
Across the snow evenly printed
A string, paw upon paw, exactly,

As if but one pad left a track there....

(lines 223-319)
Then Michal gave a startled shudder,
Looked across the Nioman, huddled
Crouched behind a fir-tree, greedy-
Eyed, and unslung his shot-gun, speedy,
Excited, trembling, for he sees
A fierce wolf from the village flees;
Straight for Michal the wolf is heading!
With joy the man's heart started thudding:
'Wait, brother, wait, old wolf! I'm making
A welcome for you, no mistaking!'
The wolf runs, tearing the snow quickly,
Only his tail is all a-flicker,
Someone has frightened him already.
Michal within himself is saying.
The wolf flies. Look, he's on the river...
Behind the hill he's disappeared,
Five minutes more, and he'll be here.
'Stop now, aim steady, not a quiver!'
Michal stood stock-still, never blinking:
It will be soon now, he is thinking.
Soon, soon the brute will be seen, surely!...
Somehow the tension's too long-drawn, though –
He is not here, he's overdue.
What is the matter? What to do?
Michal gets up, looks all about him,
As if he'd lost something, sad, doubting,
And his hands tremble. If at least
He could but frighten the great beast!
But where is he, that son of Satan?
Michal is seized by agitation,

Does not know where to cast his sight;
He cuts across, looks to the right:
Will he find him in that direction?
If not, he'll make a close inspection
Of the snow, but all in vain:
There are no tracks there, it is plain.
He runs back – No! He's gone entirely!
On Michal falls a strange perspiring.
Towards the Nioman now he hurried,
And when he looked, in dread he shuddered,
Everything in him trembled, quaking,
He nearly lost his cap with shaking,
Michal saw why: the ice had opened,
And in the gap the wolf fought, groping!
He saw Michal – his teeth were gnashing,
And furiously his eyes were flashing.

Then Michal grabbed his gun, and gamely
At the wolf took careful aim, then
Lowered the gun, thoughtfully, slowly,
And at the wolf he looked more closely.
He is right here, why, you could touch him,
At the pit's edge his paws are clutching;
The crack is deep, the ice slopes steeply,
Slashed by the water, the poor creature
At the ice with his claws is scrabbling,
Thrusts his nose at it, teeth tear, grabbing,
He is all tense, struggling and flailing,
His efforts, though, are not availing,
And the wolf's strength grows ever weaker.
But death is dread and life lures sweetly!
He gathers up his strength's last leavings,
Still harder on his paws he's heaving,

But there is nothing left to grip now,
The paws grow weaker still, they slip now.
They scratch the ice but hardly dent it,
At the very brink still straining –
No shadow of a hope remaining
In this his last sad dread adventure --
Poor wolf, no one case save you! Fruitless
Your struggles are – all, all is useless!
Your strength cannot prolong much longer
The fight; the current grows still stronger.
The wolf is weaker, almost frozen,
The current grips him, he is losing,
But, struggling with the stream still stoutly,
Slowly he turned his head about him,
His eye toward Michal now raising,
No longer with fierce anger glaring,
He seemed to seek for help, despairing,
And – only pity met his gazing!
From his eyes stared such sadness mute,
No one would have the heart to shoot!

Once more the poor wolf tried to struggle,
Then on his back turned of a sudden,
Gave one brief mournful howl, rolled, wallowed,
Log-like beneath the ice was swallowed!
And all was gone – life, the undaunted
Struggle, all the lust for hunting.
Michal stood up then, sadly pondered,
Then lifting up his head, half-wondered,
As if he had a question keen
(Though there was no one to be seen):
 'Well, brother, what d'you say to this?'

XX. YULETIDE

(lines 1-26)
Philip-tide. Then St Nicholas.
More merrily the days now pass.
For thought the winter presses harshly,
And its dread chill rages vastly
Like some wild and savage revel.
And the wind howls and whistles ever
Like clarinet or bagpipe wailing
At some monstrous banquet playing –
Yet eyes of distances gleam brightly,
And their garments glisten whitely.
Beauty dwells in those winters chilly,
And in the dead-white of their kilims
That hang and shimmer as with crystals.
Over the dumbstruck forests glistening,
When frost on fiery throne is seated,
With tapestries all crimson-bleeding,
And o'er the world his hands he raises,
Quietly enchanting and embracing
Or when the blizzard swells in power,
And winds wax stronger with snow-showers,
And all things tremble in white whirlwind...
What freedom's there in that bold swirling!
It's your hour, winter, revel, larking!
Soon Candlemas, the half-way mark, comes.
The warmth will start to blow you from us,
Bright sun by day begin to warm us.
....

XXIV. EASTER

(lines 82-120)
… Above the quiet grey earth extended
The festal night-time hung, suspended;
It was peaceful pleasant weather,
It seemed nature itself could under-
Stand the feast's dignity and wonder,
With people in accord together.
The conifers were quiet, no frisson
Of sound from the pine-wood musician,
It stood in silence, meditating
It seemed, for Easter quietly waiting.
'All terrors have quite disappeared now'
Kastuś heard whispered in his ear, now
From joyful thought of the great feast-day,
The beasts feel it, the birds feel Easter,
The fir-trees feel it, the spruce wood, too,
And evil folk have all turned good, too,
All things with God's blest feast are breathing,
No robber now will dare, deceiving,
To crouch with drawn blade by the roadway.
For now the mighty and the lowly
Keep Easter's holy celebration
And in their hearts feel jubilation.
This concord and this joy unflagging
Kastuś perceived in all around him,
In his uncle's talk it sounded,
Gossiping with Dad upon the waggon,
And in his brother's questions, chatting,
In woods still voiceless and unspeaking,
Felt it in the woods' measured creaking,
For you could feel the roadway even

Obeys God's will in this great season
And passes on the wondrous tidings
To the wheels so loudly riding.
Out of the woods the road is going
Across the ploughland; wheels are slowing
Through the loose sand scrunching, hissing,
And there it is now, in the distance,
The village church, with lantern beaming,
Lighting wayfarers with its gleaming.

XXX. THE DEATH OF MICHAL

(lines 1-79)
The end… A word so simple-seeming,
Yet ever new and multi-meaninged!
How often, 'neath the cross of fortune,
In the soul's pangs, we raise imploring
Hands and eyes filled with strange burning,
For liberation's instant yearning!
A happy instant – gone are fetters.
The end – and some closed circle shatters
Into non-being, goes for ever
Yielding its place unto another,
Time, and the faith in that end fated
Destroy decay's sepulchral sating.

The end… how much of meditation,
And how much sad deliberation
Lies in this word, simple and doomful,
In divers forms and aspects looming,
When, a last boundary, is seen to
Stand the end, firmset between you

And all that you know dearest, sweetest,
That fired your spirit and set beating
The heart with power uncanny, magic,
Like a hymn on the lips of rapids,
That, in the turbulent water's voices,
Where the sun with itself rejoices,
Murmurs full-vigoured, murmurs freely,
Bell-like chiming, white-foam-seething.

And you too, my dear narration,
Mirror of life and meditation,
A simple fate, traced firm for ever,
Where echoes of truth and freedom quiver
Eternal, you see twilight yonder
Already, the lute's timid chiming
Grows quiet, your day's silent declining
Draws near, your last steps now you wander.
And I am grieved: I lived together
With you, with one thought, one soul ever,
I carried you in a mother's fashion,
Who carries the child's unclear impression.
And you, it seems, have not been born in
A happy time to this world's storming,
For still the spring is far far distant,
Behind a wall well-builded hidden,
Captive in a dread prison pining,
While over us the siege of night-time
Hangs in a darkness thick, oppressing,
And with a heavy heel is pressing,
Like an attack (and none can fight it)
On all that gave to life new brightness.
And while the night was passing slowly,
And, all-in-all, life rotted wholly,

And then the road, the road before us,
Parting with homeland, fears hang o'er us,
And then the wandering, forced upon us,
And the weary struggle onwards
For interest of life still yearning,
And then, the foeman's heel returning.

How often lived we, my narration,
Through fleeting hour of separation
From native land, an hour of grieving,
Joy's instant, inspiration giving!
The soul burned then with holy fire,
With concord, harmony suspired,
Blending mysterious music secret,
And then was heard the grain-ears' speaking,
In native furrows, distant ringing,
And bright-eyed reaping-maiden's singing,
The sight of hills, steep-sided clinging,
Of groves and shaggy-headed pine-trees,
All so gentle, all so kindly,
Like a good-hearted old grandmother,
They warmed the heart and drew it thither,
Before the eyes they stood, as living,
The speaking strings were all aquiver,
They played in harmony united,
Upon unseen tablets writing
Three words that never flowered to life;
Runes of the ages they inscribed…
And so the farewell hour is coming,
And the last step of your long roaming!
…………………………………………..

(lines 223-260)
Alone Michal kept warm the striving,
The cause to due completion driving,
But, unbeknownst and all unnoticed,
Ill-luck prepared, its nets were woven
To throw upon Michal, to snare him,
Heeding naught and for naught caring,
Like an enchantment maleficient.
Then, by chance, Michal grew suspicious:
Saw thick smears of red blood coming!
"Eh, brother, here's a sorry omen!
The end for Michal and no error!"
He thought it a strange kind of terror.
Even the heart was failing in him.
What was it, truly, had come on him?
Was this death truly, come untimely?
No, no! Too soon to think of dying!
Michal was dread-struck. Melancholy
And the dark scroll of illness wholly
Wraps him round in all his being.
He feels alone in this world, seeing
Hostile fates and their power, staring
Into his eyes, unlovely glaring,
And rising in dread battlementing,
Twixt life and him, Michal, preventing.
Now, for the first time, he felt the anguish
Of that dread moment, past withstanding,
That lies for all in ambush waiting;
Death is an evil past escaping.
"And must I die, and shall this body
Rot in the earth, a scar unlovely
Upon the earth's fair body laid?"
And there pressed terrifying shades

Upon the heart, upon the spirit.
And then, as clear as in a mirror,
He saw the seals of death before him,
And all its phantoms, clearly forming;
He felt he was a dust-mote only,
And human life a single moment.
. . . .

(lines 314-333)
For some time now, since winter's coming,
In the strong grip of illness struggled
Michal, an illness evil, heavy,
Undesired and unexpected.
Worse still: this sickness had been coming
For a long time, not just since summer,
And from this fact its might was growing,
That it came stealthily, unnoticed,
For several years it came on, creeping,
And in the grog-shops found good feeding,
Till it had spread its fill, then mighty
It struck Michal down swiftly smiting.
At first Michal tried to resist it,
Would not surrender to this sickness,
Then to a course of cures he hurried,
(Most from a home apothecary!)
He drank tisanes and herbal potions;
They did not good to his condition.
And, far too late for such a case,
They took to the doctors poor Michaś.
. . . .

(lines 567-637)
Michal struggles in fear, and utters
A cry, the curtain slightly flutters,
His eyes he opens with an effort –
Against his hand a hand is pressing,
And someone's eyes, all filled with pain there,
To his own blurring eyes seem chained there.
No strength is left to struggle longer,
With deep regret, with trembling horror,
He calls to those around to save him,
Brother, children, wife to aid him.
But heaven waits, deafly, severely,
Will not incline an ear to hear you,
No matter how you beg and plead,
Tear your breast, pluck the heart from in it,
You will not melt its harshness, win it,
No matter how you intercede –
It is far off; dumb and unmoving,
Silent it is, and empty proving.
"Michaś, my dearest, do you know me?"
He lifts his eyes, painfully, slowly;
He sees his wife there. "Hanna… Mother…
Give me your help now!... O my brother!
Help me! Help me, my children dearest!"
And bitter as gall or wormwood, tears are
There, from the eyes deep-sunken flowing…
Michal sighs – his voice lower, lower…
"Quick, the blest candle! Quick, he's going!"
Face marked with lines that anguish wreaked there;
His hands upon his breast fell weakly,
And Michal once more shuddered, shaking,
And once more his eyes fluttered open,
It seems there's something must be spoken,

Deeply he sighs, his breath is failing,
Then suddenly, he sees it plainly:
"Antoś!... I'm dying... Brother dearest!...
I've burned out... I am disappearing...
You are in charge... the only one...
My brother best... like my own son.
God did not grant that I know freedom,
In my own furrow cast the seed in...
The land... the land... there, brother... forward,
Build on it... give it proper order...
Live a new way... secure... and steady...
Don't leave them! Ah-ah – I ... am... ready!..."
No living words, the heart-beat vanished,
Antoś the cooling hand in anguish
Kisses with bitter sobbing, groaning,
Falling upon the body, moaning.

In the field, in the field,
By the path drooping,
 There leans a cross,
O'er a grave stooping.

The pathways run far,
To the wide world tending,
They lead back home,
To this dear grave wending ...

O, you pathways of human kind, you
Narrow tracks, you pathways winding!
You stumble on your way unsurely,
Wandering as if dense woods hung o'er you,
The highway with broad stream allures you,
The rosy-blue horizon draws you,

Where sunlight pleasantly is gleaming,
Where thought upon its loom is weaving,
Thus to weave a new world of life,
To give the heart peace, rest from strife.
And banish its deep cares forever! ...
O spacious highway, when, O when,
Will you bloom in the world of men,
Drawing our every road together.

NOTES

p. 79 *The New Land*, a long, largely
autobiographical, narrative poem in several
chapters was written and published in parts
between 1911 and 1923. The first eight
chapters were written when Kolas was in prison
for nationalist activities in 1908 – hence the
keynote of exiled longing in the opening
sections.
[editorial addition: the head of the family at the
centre of the poem is Michal (sometimes
shortened to Michaś). Next to him is his brother
Anton (Antoś). Michal's wife is Hanna. We
learn from Part III of the poem ('At table') that
Michal and Hanna have four sons and three
daughters. In the parts translated by Vera, we
learn that the sons are called Kanstancin (also
Kastuś or Kostuś)[Kolas himself], Aliaksandar
(Alieś), Uladzimier (Uladzik) and Jazep
(Juzik)[Joseph].]

p. *81 part I.* 'Until they poured into the
Nioman': the Nioman is a major river in the
west of Belarus. It flows to the sea through
Lithuania.

p. *82* 'on fence-post propped to dry, a
pitcher': a typical Belarusian scene.
Earthenware pots, jugs and similar vessels after
scouring were inverted over the 'head' of a
fence-post to dry.

p. 83 'a yeoman-peasant maiden': the literal meaning of the Belarusian words is noble peasants. Yeoman-peasants were descendants of those peasants who in the olden feudal days of the Grand Duchy of Lithuania lived on crown lands held directly from the ruler. They were free of all feudal duty save military service in time of war. Following the emancipation act of 1861 in the Russian Empire, there remained no legal difference between yeoman-peasants and the ordinary variety (the former serfs). Nevertheless, the yeoman-peasant villages tended to hold themselves aloof from the bulk of the population, to whom their often pathetic attempts to live according to a style they could no longer afford were a regular source of humour.

p. 83 'the Catholic Chapel': Kolas here uses a Belarusian word that comes from Polish specifically meaning 'Catholic church'. By using this word here Kolas adds to the overall impression that the 'yeoman-peasant maiden' is trying to ape the manners and airs of a Polish gentlewoman with umbrella and sweeping train of skirts.

p. 83 part II. The culinary descriptions in this section become clearer once the reader knows that Belarusian pancakes are baked in the oven, not fried in a pan.

p. 84   *kvas*: a weak alcoholic drink fermented from rye bread rusks soaked in water.

p. 89   *part VI.* Parečča is the name of several villages in Belarus. (The name simply means 'the territory by the river'.) The village to which Kolas is actually referring is Lastok in Minsk Province, where he spent his boyhood years.

p. 89   'One to the forest, one the…..': Vera was obviously searching for the meaning of one Belarusian word in this sentence, 'adbor'. Ordinarily the word means 'selection', but in this context it is likely to mean that this particular son of Michal has gone off to attend to a variety of clearing up jobs in the forest.

p. 89   'And forty seven in cash, also': forty seven roubles.

p. 89   *part VIII.* This brief extract contains the first mention of Michal's dream for himself and his family – to buy his own land, the New Land of the poem's title.

p. 92   *part XVI.* Part XVI was written shortly after the Peace of Riga (1921) between Poland and Soviet Russia. Belarus was partitioned; the western part of the country was incorporated into the re-established Polish state.

p. 98   part XX. 'Philip-tide': the period of the Nativity Fast observed in the Eastern Orthodox and Eastern Catholic churches, between the Feast of St Philip the Apostle in November and Christmas.

p. 100   part XXX. Three words that never flowered to life': the three
words are 'My native nook' – the opening words of the poem (see p. 79)

p. 103 The 'striving' is the effort to purchase 'the new land' – the search for which is the major theme of the epic.

p. 104 'Seals of death': This may be a reference to Revelations 6-8, or, more probably, it is an image of an official seal on a legal document (the red colour of the wax being evoked by the thick colour of the blood which is the final, and condemning symptom of the illness). If the latter alternative is the poet's intention, then, since such a wax seal would have appeared, in particular, on the deed of purchase of the 'new land', we have a strong example of tragic irony.

p. 105 "Quick, the blest candle! Quick, he's going!":
a candle, blessed in church on Candlemas day (2February) and kept in the house for such an emergency. In this case, the candle would be placed in the hand of the dying man.

***

MAKSIM BAHDANOVIČ

Maksim Bahdanovič (1891-1917) made an immense contribution to Belarusian literature as poet, prose writer and critic. By his introduction of such classical forms as the sonnet, elegiac distich, triolet and rondeau, forms hitherto unknown to his contemporaries, he brought a new level of European sophistication to a previously mainly rural or even peasant culture, dominated by social despair, lament and often anger. Perhaps unsurprisingly, his innovations brought some accusations of art for art's sake from Naša Niva critics, but it is notable that Bahdanovič was easily the favourite poet of Belarus's post-war émigré writers, and he continues to hold a special place in the consciousness of young poets of today. It must also be said that he was far from remote from broad societal and national concerns, and that in the course of his tragically short life he covered a large number of different themes and forms, often writing ostensibly simple verses with supreme technical mastery – what might be called the art that conceals art.

He was born in Minsk on 10 December 1891, but from the age of five lived in the Russian town of Nizhni Novgorod, where his father, a distinguished ethnographer and folklorist, taught him to read Belarusian literature, and also instilled in him love for his native folklore, something that is reflected in early poems like 'Zmiainy car' (The Serpent-King, 1910), and was to find more sophisticated expression in his 'Vieršy bielaruskaha skladu' (Poems of the Belarusian Type, 1918), which combined popular and legendary subjects with an attempt at a specifically Belarusian type of apparently simple yet formally refined versification.

In the summer of 1911 Bahdanovič made a long-anticipated visit to Belarus, where acquaintance with the history, artefacts and physical environment of his native country, resulted in two important verse cycles, 'Miesta' (The Town, 1911-12), which conveys the excitement and bustle of pre-war Vilnia, rather than depicting towns as places where country dwellers may be subjected to mockery and exploitation; and 'Staraja Bielaruś (Old Belarus, 1913), the opening poem of which, 'Lietapisiec' (The Chronicler), tells of the devious and obscure paths by which history is transmitted. This is just one of the poems translated by Vera Rich from the works of Bahdanovič, with whom she appears to have felt a particular affinity.

In fact, many of this poet's works are extremely well known, having been set to music by a number of composers, no doubt attracted by their inherent musicality. Such verses include 'Ramans' (Romance, 1913) as 'Zorka Vieniera', and 'Sluckija tkačychi' (The Weaver-Girls of Sluck, 1912) and 'Liavonicha' (1915-16), both with the same title as in the original poems.

Bahdanovič's innovative verse forms doubtless came from his extensive reading and masterly translations of the works of classical and oriental writers and of several Russian, Ukrainian and other poets, especially Heinrich Heine and Paul Verlaine. It is notable that the subjects of some of the poems in classical forms are far from abstract: for instance, the triolet to Siarhiej Palujan, 'S.E. Palujanu' (1909), is about life passing like smoke, but memory living eternally, which perhaps gains extra pathos from the fact that the highly talented Palujan took his own life in the following year. Another triolet, 'Kaliś hliadzieǔ na sonca ja...' (Once I gazed at the sun..., 1913' shows a person who, though blinded, has a message for those who mock him. The rondeau of 1911, 'Uzor pryhožy pieknych zor...' (Design of stars so fair and fine...) encapsulates within tightly wrought form one of Bahdanovič's principal aesthetic ideas, namely the frequent unlikeliness of natural sources of real beauty.

Although Bahdanovič, like his contemporaries, was capable of rousing calls to his fellow-countrymen, nonetheless delicacy and pathos are important both in his lyrics as well as cycles like 'Madonny' (Madonnas, 1913) with its immensely touching poem 'U vioscy' (In the Village). Strong examples of the poet's ability to arouse genuine sentiment include, 'Sluckija tkačychi' where the weavers dream of their native villages, introducing a Belarusian cornflower into their Persian patterns, and 'Jak Bazylí u pachodzie kanaŭ...' (When Basil died, far on the march..., 1915), in which are described his last wistful dreams of Belarus and its native beauty. These poems are amongst the most affecting of all Belarusian works written at this time.

When he died of tuberculosis in the Crimea on 12 May 1917 renascent Belarusian literature was dealt a cruel blow indeed.

Prof. Arnold McMillin
London

Раманс

> *Quand luira cette étoile, un jour,*
> *La plus belle et la plus lointaine,*
> *Dites-lui qu'elle eut mon amour,*
> *O derniers de la race humaine.*
>
> Sully-Prudhomme

Зорка Венера ўзышла над зямлёю,
Светлыя згадкі з сабой прывяла...
Помніш, калі я спаткаўся з табою,
Зорка Венера ўзышла.

З гэтай пары я пачаў углядацца
Ў неба начное і зорку шукаў.
Ціхім каханнем к табе разгарацца
З гэтай пары я пачаў.

Але расстацца нам час наступае;
Пэўна, ўжо доля такая у нас.
Моцна кахаў я цябе, дарагая,
Але расстацца нам час.

Буду ў далёкім краю я нудзіцца,
Ў сэрцы любоў затаіўшы сваю;
Кожную ночку на зорку дзівіцца
Буду ў далёкім краю.

Глянь іншы раз на яе, – у расстанні
Там з ёй зліём мы пагляды свае...
Каб хоць на міг уваскрэсла каханне,
Глянь іншы раз на яе...

1912

Romance

Venus new-risen above us appearing
Brings with her bright-shining memories of love;
Do you recall when I first met, my dear one,
Venus new-risen above?
From that time forth evermore, skyward gazing
Seeking that planet I'd scan heaven o'er,
Within me a deep silent love for you blazing,
From that time forth, evermore.
But the time of our parting draws near, ever nearer,
Thus does our fate, does our fortune appear.
Deeply, profoundly I love you, my dearest,
But the time of our parting draws near.
In that far country, my love buried deeply,
I shall live drearily, yet, high above
I shall gaze on that planet each night, vigil keeping,
In that far country, my love!
Gaze upon Venus once more, when far distant
One from another, there mingling we'll pour
Our glances, let love flower again for an instant...
Gaze upon Venus once more!

Летапісец

Душой стаміўшыся ў жыццёвых цяжкіх бурах,
Свой век канчае ён у манастырскіх мурах.
Тут ціша, тут спакой -- ні шуму, ні клапот.
Ён пільна летапіс чацвёрты піша год
І спісвае усё ад слова і да слова
З даўнейшых граматак пра долю Магілёва.
І добрыя яго, і кепскія дзяла
Апавядае тут. Так рупная пчала
Умее ў соты мёд зыбраць і з горкіх кветак,
І бачанаму ім – ён годны веры сьведак.
Што тут чынілася у даўнія гады,
Што думалі, аб чым спрачаліся тады,
За што змагаліся, як баранілі веру, –
Узнаюць гэта ўсё патомкі праз паперу!
Яно забудзецца, умрэ, з вадой сплыве, –
І вось у спомінах устане, ажыве,
Калі знайдуць яго няхітрае пісаньне
Пра гэтае жыццё, надзеі, справаванне...
Так мора сіняе прымчыць да нас вадой
Бутэльку к берагу, аблітую смалой,
Ўсю ў дробных ракаўках і ў ціне. Не замала
Яна была ў вадзе і шмат чаго спаткала.
Рыбалкі вылавяць бутэльку, разаб'юць
І, як трапляецца, быць мо у ёй знайдуць
Ліста. Па звычаю марскому гэтак весці
Нам, утапаючы, шлюць людзі. Ў моры гдзесьці
Загінулі яны, і, можа, сотні год
З тых часаў працяклі, і згінуў іх народ,
І ўсё змянілася, і ўжо пра іх забылі.
Вы, літары, цяпер нанова ўсё збудзілі!

І людзі зведаюць аб прадзедах сваіх, --
Аб горы, радасцях і аб прыгодах іх,
Каму маліліся, чаго яны шукалі,
Дзе на глыбокім дне іх крыюць мора хвалі.

1912

The Chronicler

His soul grown weary-tired in life's stern tempests fending,
Within cloister walls his days he now is ending.
Here is silence, here is calm -- no hubbub and no noise.
Copying a chronicle four years he has employed.
Copying the whole from an ancient parchment,
From first word to the last, of Mahilou and what passed
there.
And here are deeds of good and ill-deeds equally
Set in the record. Just so the industrious bee
Even from bitter flowers can fill its combs with honey.
Then of events he saw he adds true testimony.
Here are the things which came to pass in former ages,
What men thought then, and of what disputed sagely,
Why they fought, and how the true faith they defended --
By this paper all made known to their descendants!
All is long-forgotten, dead, on waters drifting --
But now it will arise, once more in memory living,
When they find his simple, unadorned narration,
Telling of that life, its hopes, its expectation.
Just so the blue sea carries to the shore
To us a little flask where resin once was poured,
Covered with small mussel shells and mud. Long, truly,
It lay in the water, much it did endure there;
Some fishermen may find the bottle, stave it in,
And, so it happens, they may find there is, within,
A letter. By the custom of the sea, some message
Sent by shipwrecked sailors. Somewhere they have perished
In the ocean; maybe centuries rolled on
Since that time, maybe the nation now is gone,
And all is changed, and even memory is drowsing!

But, letters, you once more will waken and arouse men,
And then about their forebears they will learn, and read
About their woes and joys, about their noted deeds,
To whom they made their prayer, what for they were
seeking,
Where on the deep sea floor the waves forever keep them.

Слуцкія ткачыхі

Ад родных ніў, ад роднай хаты
У панскі двор дзеля красы
Яны, бяздольныя, узяты
Ткаць залатыя паясы.
І цягам доўгія часіны,
Дзявочыя забыўшы сны,
Свае шырокія тканіны
На лад персідскі ткуць яны.
А за сцяной смяецца поле,
Зіяе неба з-за акна, –
І думкі мкнуцца мімаволі
Туды, дзе расцвіла вясна;
Дзе блішча збожжа ў яснай далі,
Сінеюць міла васількі,
Халодным срэбрам ззяюць хвалі
Між гор ліючайся ракі;
Цямнее край зубчаты бора...
І тчэ, забыўшыся, рука,
Заміж персідскага узора,
Цвяток радзімы вasілька.

1912

The Weaver-Girls of Slucak

From native home, from native tillage,
To the Big House, for beauty's sake,
Luckless girls taken from their village,
Girdles of woven gold to make.
Long hours of labour they endeavour,
Forgetful of their girlish dreams,
Toiling at the broad weaving ever.
Where the Persian pattern gleams.
Outside the walls is smiling tillage,
The sky shines fair beyond the pane,
And thoughts go wandering, willy-nilly,
There where the spring's in flower again.
There by the rye, in the far distance,
The cornflowers gleam with azure still,
And waves of chilly silver glisten,
Where rivers gush between the hills;
Dark frowns the forest's jagged verdure,
And hands, forgetful at the loom,
Neglecting the designs of Persia,
Weave in the native cornflower bloom.

Санет

Un sonnet sans défaut veut un long poème
Boileau

Паміж пяскоў Егіпецкай зямлі,
Над хвалямі сінеючаго Ніла,
Ўжо колькі тысяч год стаіць магіла:
Ў гаршчку насення жменю там знайшлі.
Хоць зернейкі засохшымі былі,
Усё ж такі жыццёвая іх сіла
Збудзілася і буйна ўскаласіла
Парой вясенняй збожжа на раллі.

Вось сімвал твой, забыты краю родны!
Зварушаны нарэшце дух народны,
Я верую, бясплодна не засне,
А ўперад рынецца, маўляў крыніца,
Каторая магутна, гучна мкне,
Здалеўшы з глебы на прастор прабіцца.

1911

Sonnet

Where the Egyptian sands spread far around,
Close where the waves of azure Nile are flowing,
A tomb stood many thousand years: men going
Within, some seeds hid in a jar were found.
Although the grains were parched and dried, still sound
Their vital force awoke, and, new life knowing,
Flourished abundantly, young ears were growing,
In spring the crop stood high above the ground.

Forgotten land of mine, this is your symbol;
At last thy people's spirit is atremble,
I believe it lies not in sterile sleep,
But that it will surge upward like a fountain,
Which, rushing in a mighty, sounding leap,
Pierces the soul, into free spaces mounting.

Эміграцкая песня

Ёсць на свеце такія бадзягі,
Што не вераць ні ў Бога, ні ў чорта.
Ім прыемны стракатыя сцягі
Караблёў акіянскага порта.

І няма ім каго тут пакінуць,
Бо нікога на свеце не маюць.
Ўсё ім роўна: ці жыць, ці загінуць, —
Аднаго яны моцна жадаюць:

Пабываць у краях незнаёмых,
Ды зазнаць там і шчасця і гора,
І загінуць у хвалях салёных
Белапеннага сіняга мора.

Але мы — не таго мы шукаем,
Не таго на чужыне нам трэба.
Не рассталіся б мы з нашым краем,
Каб было дзеля нас у ім хлеба.

І на вулцы пад грукат, пад гоман,
Дзе натоўп закруціўся рухавы,
Нам маячыцца вёсачка, Нёман
І агні партавыя Лібавы.

1914

Emigrants' Song

There are in this world such far-rovers
Who believe not in God nor in devil,
Who delight in bright banners high over
The ships that in ocean ports revel.

They have none here to leave whom they cherish
For they have neither kin nor belongings,
They care not if they live or they perish,
On one sole aim are fixed all their longings:

To visit lands, so far unsought-for,
To taste there of fortune and grieving,
And to perish among the salt waters
Of blue seas where white foam is heaving.

But we do not seek such a bounty,
It is not far lands we are needing,
We would not have left our dear country
If there had been bread for our feeding.

And in clatter and noise of streets roaming,
Where the crowd, ever-restless, whirls streaming,
We dream of the village, the Nioman,
And Libava with harbour lights gleaming.

"Як Базыль у паходзе канаў"

Як Базыль у паходзе канаў,
Ўсё старонку сваю спамінаў.
– Вы прашчайце, прашчайце, шнуры,
Вы прашчайце, негараныя!
Мне вас болі ужо не гараць,
Буйным збожжам на зары не засяваць.
– Не пабачу я цябе, цёмны луг,
Поле чыстае, раздольнае!
Мне па вас ужо піколі не хадзіць,
Мне зялёнай травы не касіць.
– Расстаюся я з табой, шчыры бор,
Пушча цёмная, драмучая!
Мне твой шум ужо болі не чуваць,
Мне высокіх сасон не рубаць.
– Ах, прашчай ты, сямейка мая,
Вы прашчайце, таварышы!
Ўжо пе прыйдзецца да сэрца прытуліць,
Пасядзець, пажартаваць, пагаманіць.
– Гэй, чалом табе, чалом, Беларусь,
Ўся старраначка бяздольная!
Не забыў твой сын сваей маці,
За цябе ў зямлі яму ляжаці.
· ·
Як Базыль у паходзе канаў,
Ўсё старонку сваю спамінаў.

1915

When Basil died...

When Basil died, far on the march?
He dreamed of his land at the last.
'Farewell, ah, farewell, ploughland strips,
Farewell, too, to you, unploughed fallow,
I shall never plough you again,
Nor at dawn sow a rich crop of grain,
Dark meadow, I'll not gaze on thee more,
Thou clean, broad field stretching boundlessly!
Nevermore to walk across thee shall I go,
Nevermore the green grass shall I mow.
I am leaving thee, pinewood sincere,
Dark and dreaming, forest primeval!
No longer shall I hear thee rustle so,
No more lay thy lofty pines low.
Ah, farewell to you, my dearest friends!
No more to press you close to my heart,
Sit with you, in jokes and talk take my part.
Ah, a reverent farewell, Belarus,
Thou my country all fortuneless.
Thy son does not forget his mother,
For thee he'll lie here, earth his cover...'
When Basil died far on the march,
He dreamed of his land at the last.

Лявоніха

Ах, Лявоніха, Лявоніха мая!
Спамяну цябе ласкавым словам я, —
Чорны пух тваіх загнутых брывянят,
Вочы яркія, вясёлы іх пагляд;
Спамяну тваю рухавую пастаць,
Спамяну, як ты умела цалаваць.

Ой, Лявоніха, Лявоніха мая!
Ты пяяла галасней ад салаўя,
Ты была заўсёды першай у танку —
І ў «Мяцеліцы», і ў «Юрцы», і ў «Бычку»;
А калі ты жаці станеш свой загон,
Аж дзівуецца нядбайліца Лявон.

Ой, Лявоніха, Лявоніха мая!
У цябе палова вёскі — кумаўя.
Знала ты, як запрасіць, пачаставаць,
І дарэчы слова добрае сказаць,
І разважыць, і ў смутку звесяліць,
А часамі — і да сэрца прытуліць.

Ой, Лявоніха, Лявоніха мая!
Дай жа бог табе даўжэйшага жыцця,
Дай на свеце сумным радасна пражыць,
Ўсіх вакол, як весяліла, весяліць.
Хай ніколі не забуду цябе я.
Ой, Лявоніха, Лявоніха мая!

1916

Liavonicha

O Liavonicha, Liavonicha my dear,
I remember you in loving words sincere,
I remember your curved brows' black downy haze,
I recall your bright eyes and your merry gaze,
I recall your lively form, and, more than –
I remember well that you knew how to kiss!

O Liavonicha, Liavonicha my dear,
You sang louder than the nightingale to hear,
In the dance you always took the foremost place,
'Snowstorm', 'Jurca', 'Bull-calf jig' – you set the pace,
And at harvest time, so boldly reaped you on,
That it quite astonished your no-good Liavon!

O Liavonicha, Liavonicha my dear,
Half the village are your gossips; it is clear
You know how to welcome guests – a hostess gay –
You've learned always just the proper things to say,
How to cheer, and how to make dull grief depart,
And, in season, how to press friends to your heart.

O Liavonicha, Liavonicha my dear,
May God grant your life be long and never drear,
May you live in joy among this world so sad,
As you once brought gladness, so may you be glad,
May my memories of you ne'er disappear,
O Liavonicha, Liavonicha my dear.

З цыкла "Мадонны"

Lumen coeli, sancta rosa
Aleksandr Pushkin

I

У ВЁСЦЫ

Хвалююць сэрца нам дзявочыя пастаці,
І душы мацярэй нас могуць чараваці;
Вышэйшая краса -- ў іх злітнасці жывой!
Артысты-маляры схіляліся прад ёй,
Жадаючы з'явіць цераз свае халсціны
Пачуцці мацеры у вобліку дзяўчыны.
Красы тэй сімвалам, маць-дзева, стала ты, -
І глянулі твае з-пад пэндзаляў чэрты.
З таемным трэпетам на іх я пазіраю,
А сэрца ўсё імкне да бацькаўскага краю.
Мінулае сваё прыпамінаю я!
Між цёмных абразкоў прайшоўшага жыцця
Шукаю сквапна штось трывожнаю душою,
І здаранне адно ўстае перада мною.

Калісьці летняю рабочаю парой
Праз вёску я ішоў. Панураю чаргой
З абох бакоў крывой і вузкай вулкі хаты
Стаялі -- шэрыя, струхлеўшыя; як латы,
Віднеліся ў сцянах сляпыя вокны іх,

І аж счарнелася салома стрэх гнілых.
Ўсё руйнавалася, старэла, адмірала,
І мала што вакол хоць трохі аздабляла
Вясковую нуду: мак яркія цвяткі
Рознакалёрныя, як тыя матылькі,
У градах высыпаў і цешыў імі душу,
Ды можна йшчэ там-сям пабачыць грушу,
Крывую, старую... вось толькі і ўсяго.
І да таго ж з людзей не відна нікаго, --
Яны на полі ўсе; не мільканець спадніца,
Не пройдзе з вёдрамі па воду маладзіца,
Не ўгледзіш белую магерку мужыка,
Ў паветры не памкне іржанне жарабка,
І песня сумная не паліецца звонка...
Што ж дзіўнага, калі, раптоўна крык дзіцёнка
Пачуўшы, дрогнуў я і аглядзеўся. Ах!
Я спудзіў хлопчыка; на руках і нагах
Ён, бедненькі, папоўз па траўцы ля сцяжынкі,
Да нянькі трапляючы -- так год васьмі дзяўчынкі,
І вось, дабраўшыся, ў падолак разам к ей
З трывожным голасам уткнуўся ён хутчэй;
І, як схіляецца ад ветру верх бярозкі,
Дзяўчынка к хлопчыку пагнулася і, слёзкі
Сціраючы яму, штось пачала казаць,
Каб заспакоіць плач -- зусім як быццам маць,
І салівалася ў жывы абраз ядыны
Той выгляд мацеры ды з воблікам дзяўчыны,
Дзіцячым, цененькім; і ў гэты час яна
Здавалася, была аж да краёў паўна
Якойсь шырокаю, радзімаю красою,
І помню, я на міг пахарашэў душою.
А можа, не краса была ў дзяўчыны той, --
Дзяўчынцы ўпэцканай, і хілай, і худой, --

А штось вышэйшае, што Рафаэль вялікі
Стараўся выявіць праз Маці Божай лікі.

Старніца лепшая ў штодзённіку жыцця!
Зноў з ціхай радасцю цябе чытаю я.
Хай шмат чаго ўжо з тых гадоў крыніва змыла
У памяці маёй, хай тэй дзяўчынкі мілай
Ўжо воблік губіцца у цёмнай глыбіне,
Я веру, ў цяжкі час ён гляне на мяне.

From *The Madonnas*

I

IN THE VILLAGE

Beauty of young maidens sets the heart a-dancing,
And the souls of mothers have power to entrance us;
Higher beauty when they merge in living grace!
Artists, painters ever bow before its face,
Striving always through their canvas to discover
In a maiden's face the devotion of a mother...
Thou, O Virgin-Mother, art that beauty's sign –
From beneath the brush Thy holy features shine.
And I gaze on them in mystic trepidation,
My heart striving for the land of my own nation.
And I recollect all my long-past years!
Among my past life's images, dark and drear,
As I, eager, seek, with soul perturbed and stormy,
One event of long ago appears before me.

Once upon a working day in summer-time
I passed through a village. In a dreary line
On both sides of the winding narrow lane, the houses
Stood there, grey, decayed, like old rags, dull and frowsty;
In the walls their windows staring blindly back,
And even the thatch itself was rotted black.
All was ruins, grown old; here death had come crawling,
Only here and there was something still adorning

The village dreariness. The poppy still unfurled
Bright flowers like butterflies, where many colours swirled,
Beside the path, and with them made the soul grow carefree.
Then, too, one might notice here and there a pear-tree
Crooked, gnarled with age... and that, indeed. Was all --
But no one to be seen, no people, none at all -
All in the fields. No trace of bright skirt for a moment,
No new bride passed with pails to bear the water homeward,
No white caps of peasants to be seen, nowhere,
No sound of colts' neighing echoed in the air,
No sad song was heard, floating, ringing, flying...
Then, how strange! There came the sound of infant crying!
Hearing this, I started and looked round. Alas!
I'd scared a little boy; he crawled upon the grass
Beside the path, on hands and knees, poor little baby,
Towards his nursemaid - she a girl of eight years, maybe -
And now he'd reached her, and into her lap straightway
He hid his little head, voice fearful with dismay,
And, as the tip of a small birch nods in the breezes,
The girl bent to the little boy to calm and ease him,
And wiped his tears and started murmuring to him,
Exactly as a mother would. And thus within
One living form, the two mingled and merged together,
The stature of a girl, the manner of a mother.
At that moment she, childlike in form and thin,
Suddenly appeared filled to the very brim
With some far-reaching native loveliness within her,
And, I recall, my soul grew finer for an instant.
But maybe indeed it was not loveliness -
In that thin grubby puny little girl expressed -
But something higher which great Rafael endeavoured
To show in the features of Our Lord's own Mother.

A better page thou art in my life's diary!
I read you once again quiet and joyfully.
Let many of these years be borne off by the freshet,
Let in the dark abyss the lovely features perish
Of this sweet little girl, lost from my memory,
Yet I believe in hardship's hour they'll gaze on me.

Пагоня

Толькі ў сэрцы трывожным пачую
За краіну радзімую жах, -
Ўспомню Вострую Браму святую
І ваякаў на грозных канях.

Ў белай пене праносяцца коні,
Рвуцца, мкнуцца і цяжка хрыпяць -
Старадаўняй Літоўскай Пагоні
Не разбіць, не спыніць, не стрымаць.

У бязмерную даль вы ляціце,
А за вамі, прад вамі - гады.
Вы за кім у пагоню спяшыце?
Дзе шляхі вашы йдуць і куды?

Мо яны, Беларусь, панясліся
За тваімі дзяцьмі ўздагон,
Што забылі цябе, адракліся,
Прадалі і аддалі ў палон?

Біце ў сэрцы іх - біце мячамі,
Не давайце чужынцамі быць!
Хай пачуюць, як сэрца начамі
Аб радзімай старонцы баліць.

Маці родная, Маці-краіна!
Не усцішыцца гэтакі боль…
Ты прабач, Ты прымі свайго сына,
За Цябе яму ўмерці дазволь!..

Ўсё лятуць і лятуць тыя коні,
Срэбнай збруяй далёка грымяць…
Старадаўняй Літоўскай Пагоні
Не разбіць, не спыніць, не стрымаць.

Pahonia

Whensoever my anxious heart, trembling
With fear for our land, starts to bleed,
The Vostraja Gate I remember,
And the warriors on their dread steeds.

Flecked with white foam, those steeds, onward straining,
Gallop and charge, grimly snort...
Pahonia of Old Lithuania,
None can conquer them, stay them or halt.

Into measureless distances flying,
Behind you, before, years extend...
After whom do ye chase, swiftly hieing,
Where lie your paths, whither they wend?

Maybe, Belarus, they are racing
After thy sons, neglectful of thee,
Who forgot thee, thy memory effacing,
Sold, betrayed thee into slavery.

Strike them deep in the heart with swords brandished!
Let them not into foreigners turn!
Let them feel in the night their hearts' anguish
For their true native land ache and burn...

My dear Mother, my own Mother-Country,
Let there never be end to that ache...
Forgive! Take back thy son in thy bounty,
Permit him to die for thy sake!

The steeds fly and fly, onward straining,
Silver harness resounds in assault,
Pahonia of Old Lithuania,
None can conquer them, stay them or halt.

NOTES

The notes that follow are, unless otherwise specified, taken from Vera's own notes on the Bahdanovič poems in *Like Water, Like Fire*.

p.117: *Раманс/Romance*
The epigraph comes from Prudhomme's poem *L'idéal*,published in the collection *Stances et poèmes*, Paris, 1865.
Editorial note:
On her AllPoetry website page Vera added the following:
This is my translation of one of the great 'parting' poems of European literature - by the Belarusian poet Maksim Bahdanovič (1891-1917). You may perhaps find consolation in the fact that your parting need be only for a few months. His was – and he knew it was – short of a miracle, a final one as far as this world is concerned – he had tuberculosis, and – like Keats before him, was going 'south' in the hope that a warmer climate might give him a few more months of life.

p.120: *Летапісец/The Chronicler*
line 6: Mahiloŭ (Russian: Mogilyov) is an old city in the east of Belarus on the river Dniapro.

p.123: *Слуцкія ткачыхі/The Weaver-Girls of Slucak*
editorial note: This version of Vera's translation appears on her AllPoetry website page; it is later than the version in *Like Water, Like Fire*, and differs slightly from it. Slucak is now known as Sluck.
[Vera's note] This is a translation of one of the poet's most famous lyrics; it is from his cycle of poems 'Old Belarus'. The weaver-girls worked in a workshop owned by the

Radziwiłł princes in the town of Sluck, and made the broad
brocade girdles that in the 18th century formed part of the
dress of noblemen of the Polish-Lithuanian Commonwealth.
Line 20: on the basis of this poem and his 'Apocrypha' (a
short prose work written in quasi-Biblical style and language),
the cornflower is now considered to be the national flower of
Belarus.

p.127: *Эміграніцкая песня/Emigrants' Song*
The Nioman is one of the main rivers in Belarus. Libava is
now Liepāja, a Latvian port city on the Baltic.

p.129: *Як Базыль у паходзе канаў/When Basil died*
The metre of this poem is somewhat strange – each line seems
to scan as a unit, but in little relationship to adjacent lines.
Either Bahdanovič has been influenced here by Polish syllabic
metres, or the broken jerky effect is intended to indicate
the disjointed thoughts of the dying man. The alternation
of rhymed and unrhymed couplets, adding greatly to the
poignancy of this poem's 'atmosphere' inclines me to think
that the latter is the correct explanation.

p.131: *Лявоніха/Liavonicha*
The jest of this poem is that the lady's given name is *not*
Liavonicha! *Liavonicha* means simply 'wife of Liavon'; her
own name, whatever it may be, is never mentioned.
stanza 3: 'gossips' in the etymological sense of Old English
godsibb. The Slavonic relationship expressed by *kum* (fem.
kuma) includes several relationships by baptism: here,
Liavonicha will be *kuma* ('gossip') to (a) the parents of her
god-children; (b) the godfathers of her god-children, and by
extension to the wives of the godfathers of her god-children;
(c) the godparents of her own children (supposing, of course,

that she and 'no-good' Liavon have been blessed with issue!);
(d) by extension, all those persons to whom 'no-good' Liavon
is *kum*. Even allowing that group (d) will be small and group
(c) possibly non-existent, for so popular a lady as Liavonicha,
'half the village' may well be no exaggeration!

p.135: *From the cycle Мадонны/Madonnas: У вёсцы/In the Village*
The epigraph is taken from Pushkin's *Сцены из рыцарских времён* (Scenes from the Times of Knighthood).

p.140: *Пагоня/Pahonia*
Editorial note:
This is the only poem not included in *Like Water, Like Fire*.
The word 'pahonia' literally means 'chase'. It is the name of a
national emblem depicting a knight in full armour, seated on a
rearing horse, in pursuit of the enemy. It served as the emblem
of the Grand Duchy of Lithuania, a medieval and early
modern state that encompassed the territory of the modern
republics of both Lithuania and Belarus. The overwhelming
majority of its inhabitants were Slavs; there is therefore every
justification for regarding the Grand Duchy as an early form
of Belarusian statehood.
line 3: 'Vostraja Brama' (literally 'Pointed Gate') in Vilnius
is the last surviving gate to the old city. It holds a chapel
containing an icon to the Blessed Virgin May that is believed
to be miraculous and is revered by Roman Catholics and
Orthodox alike.

APPENDIX

Vera Rich paid several visits to Belarus after the country declared independence in 1991. Here are some records of her visits — including impromptu acrostic poems — of 1998, 2000 and 2007.

Prof. Viačaslaŭ Rahojša of the Belarusian State University became a good friend of Vera in the 1990s. He has made the small town of Rakaŭ, some 24 miles from Minsk, a thriving cultural centre.

Rakaŭ is the place for me,
Rakaŭ is the place to be!
Rich in learning's erudition,
Redolent of old tradition,
Right therefore it is to bring
Rhymes and lays its praise to sing.

'Athens of the North' you say,
Ah, such words could cause a fray,
Answer Scots (their brows a-furrow),
"Athens North, 'tis Edinburgh!"
Agreed, though, Rakaŭ at least
Athens is of the North East!

Kingly halls I do not need,
Kin and friends suffice indeed,
Kindly may God bless them all,
Kitchen, school, home, roof and wall,
Keep them safe, Lord, safe as snug
Kernel rests in nutshell's hug.

All the team today rejoices,
All around are happy voices,
Azure sky above us gleams,
Autumn sun pours down its beams,
And each tree, to pay due honour,
Adds a red or golden banner!

Us it then behoves to raise
Up our voice in Rakaŭ's praise.
Unity and friendship flowers
Under its twin churches' towers,
Unvexed by life's fret and fever,
Uniquely, may it live for ever!!!

Vera Rich
10/IX/1998

Rakaŭ Readings 4/XII/2000
Relentless time grinds the year down to winter,
And all around us, in the circling mists
Kindred ghosts from long ages past now glimmer,
As history, with all its subtle twists

Unites here scholars, whose discourse unfolds
Roads to a past where faiths and peoples mingle,
As colours mingle on the loom: bright golds
Kindled by joy, mauves where old sorrows tingle,

And all the subtle tints where blood and souls
Uniquely interweave in tapestry,
Rainbow threads blent in varicoloured whole –
A microcosm of true harmony.

Kindly, then, may that angel bless this home
Augustly named: Spakoj, Mir, Pax, Shalom!

Vera Rich
Вера Рыч
7/XII/2000

Greetings to the Rahojša family,
and especially to Viačaslaŭ –
whose appreciation of my version
was the first step
to my being   СТАГОДДЗЕ
accepted,   3 ДНЯ
as part of the   НАРАДЖЭННЯ
                              ЯНКІ
Belarusian   КУПАЛЫ
                          1882—1982
literary scene.

– 'The pen is mightier than the sword –
but sometimes its victories are delayed.'

Vera Rich
Rahań – 11/IX/1998

Vera at the Museum of Poetic Culture in Rakaŭ, 4.12.2000

Vera and Prof. Rahojša, 2007

www.ingramcontent.com/pod-product-compliance
Lightning Source LLC
Chambersburg PA
CBHW070822100426

42813CB00003B/452